Advance Praise for
The Power of Participation

"*The Power of Participation* provides a much-needed resource to those schools and districts that are either choosing or being required to implement site-based management including shared decision-making. I especially like how Dr. Golarz links the lofty issues of 'why' do participatory governance with the practical issues of 'how' to best proceed. His personal stories add significantly to the richness of the book."

— Dr. Lawrence W. Lezotte, Senior Vice President
Effective Schools
Okemos, Michigan

"The insights provided by the authors of this well-written and informative book represent the first serious attempt to explain the process of participatory governance. Those interested in educational reform will finally be able to have a roadmap through the maze, a map drawn with the wisdom of experience and the knowledge gained from one of our true educational pioneers."

— Dr. Phillip Harris, Director
Center for Professional Development and Services
Phi Delta Kappa
Bloomington, Indiana

"The Golarzes have provided us with a comprehensive definition of participatory governance, a solid rationale for its role in school reform, steps leading to the implementation of participatory governance in a school district, and pitfalls to watch out for during implementation. The anecdotes are expertly woven throughout the text, making it easy and enjoyable reading, yet not minimizing the importance of the work. *The Power of Participation* is a life jacket that can help school reformers take the plunge into the waters of participatory governance."

— Phedonia J. Johnson, Director
McPrep Program, The Anchor Project
Chicago, Illinois

"In educational writing, too often the author presents an idea as the one-time panacea to our educational problems. This book painstakingly nullifies this panacea notion with its emphasis on the continuance of the process of educational reform. I am drawn to Dr. Golarz because he has been a teacher, principal, and superintendent. When he speaks, or now in his writing, his knowledge and, more importantly, his application of that knowledge, adds to the book. And Mrs. Golarz, as a teacher, has influenced Dr. Golarz, as an administrator, to remain in contact with the roles of both teacher/artist and teacher/administrator."

— Ray Fulton, Director I, Leadership Development
Duval County Public Schools
Jacksonville, Florida

"*The Power of Participation* offers insight, strategy, and hope for tomorrow's schools through a major shift in the way schools are managed. Participatory governance provides a mechanism for changing the structure of public education while sustaining and promoting integrity, creativity, and the effective use of human resources. The Golarzes provide the theoretical basis, a practical implementation methodology, and the guidelines to make the process of shifting governance styles possible and successful. As an educational consultant, I will serve administrators better because of this book."

— Michelle Karns, Senior Staff Associate
National Training Associates
Sebastopol, California

"I am amazed at how *real* this book is. The authors have been in the forefront of the school reform movement for so long that they know exactly what problems to expect when implementing participatory governance as well as how schools ought to be. Their high ideals will inspire their readers."

— Dr. Gary Phillips, Director
National School Improvement Project
Issaquah, Washington

The Power
of Participation

Maria,

We have enjoyed &
learned from our time here.
glad you were a part.

Marvin

The Power of Participation

IMPROVING SCHOOLS
IN A DEMOCRATIC SOCIETY

Raymond J. Golarz
Marion J. Golarz

Research Press
2612 North Mattis Avenue
Champaign, Illinois 61821

This book was originally published by National Training Associates under the same title.

Copies of this book may be ordered from Research Press at the address given on the title page.

Developmental Editor: Emily Garfield
Copy Editor: Lorna Cunkle
Cover Designer: Paragon^3
Interior Designer: Lorna Cunkle
Printer: McNaughton & Gunn

ISBN 0–87822–360–6
Library of Congress Catalog Number 95–70526

TO OUR CHILDREN

**Tanya, Michael, Scott,
Jocelyn, Daniel, and Thomas John**

Contents

Foreword

THE EVOLUTION OF society requires that we transform the way we educate the younger generation. This perception is universally shared if we are to believe the discourses from those clearly distressed by our inability to engage all students in learning as it is currently defined. The cries for reform come from both within and outside the hallowed halls of learning.

Many people, myself included, think that until very recently we have attempted to alter education in a piecemeal fashion. We have been reacting to the barbs directed at educational institutions and come up with partial solutions rather than reexamining the educational system itself and coming up with ways to reframe educational processes. The metaphor that comes to mind is the one about the fish tank: We have been so busy focusing on the fish that we have neglected to think about the water in which they swim. I think we have also neglected to closely examine the fish tank.

Marion and Ray Golarz have captivated me — just as they will you — in their perceptive analysis of our present educational conundrum. In these pages, they review current reality and then provide us with a democratic methodology — participatory governance — that alters educational decision making. They offer instructions, to complete the metaphor, on how to redesign the fish tank and its liquid composition.

This book is a personal collaboration, a passionately written statement to all those dedicated to educational change. Reflected here are years of teaching, questioning, researching, and supervising. Shared here is the wit and wisdom of their collective experiences. For Ray, it has prompted national recognition for excellence.

Enjoy the reading, heed their advice, and laugh in the proper places!

— *Emily F. Garfield, Ph.D.*

Acknowledgments

NO BOOK, INCLUDING THIS ONE, is written in isolation. We have many friends and colleagues to thank, for it is their work, encouragement, and support that have helped us gather together and communicate the substance of our work and ideas.

The members of the staff at National Training Associates, our very own "support group," have inspired us from the beginning of this undertaking. Wayne Hunnicutt, Steve Zuieback, Lorna Cunkle, and Emily Garfield have been invaluable mentors and guides throughout our endeavor. Without their expertise in matters of content and technical procedures, this demanding process would not have been completed.

We would like to acknowledge those people in the field of education throughout the country who are so dedicated to the improvement of schools. They have inspired us with their understanding of the need to create dynamic learning environments where all community members are empowered in the effort to give children the hope and opportunity they need and deserve. The work of these people has been especially significant in our understanding of what works, what does not work, and what must work if educational improvement is to be effective.

Finally, we owe a special thanks to those with whom we have worked, lived, and served in Hammond, Hobart, and Richmond, Indiana. Without the effort of the teachers, administrators, parents, school board trustees, and community members in those cities, participatory governance would never have been given a chance. These people took personal and professional risks as they placed their trust in a new process that offered only the hope of a better way.

— RJG and MJG
November 1994

Introduction

THE MOVEMENT TOWARD participatory governance is a journey filled with potential pitfalls, for the concept itself strikes at the foundation of the well-defined, tradition-based bureaucratic organization of schools. This organization has, over the years, in every part of our country, developed customs and traditions, curricula and instructional strategies, definitions of role, status, and established practices and procedures. Flourishing around this bureaucratic network are paradigms that have been incorporated into the perceptions and expectations of the parents and students served by the institution, as well as of the staff and boards who provide the service. In fact, the institution functions so well that it can virtually carry on without direction.

Yet participatory governance has the potential to make significant changes in this tradition-based, educational bureaucracy. Participatory governance means a shift in decision-making authority and a change in the way schools are run. It impacts virtually every role performed in the organization.

This book provides the educational practitioner and community participants with the practical knowledge needed to follow a participatory governance process within an existing bureaucracy, a process that is consistent with research and founded in practical political realities. *Be forewarned, however, that the road to participatory governance can be prescriptive only in its initial phases. As more people within an organization take charge and assume responsi-*

bility for improvement, the precise evolution of change can be neither predicted nor predetermined by those who previously held the bureaucratic power.

While these pages offer much information and many guidelines, this is not a book of step-by-step instructions to a painless and orderly process. As those interested in participatory governance become immersed in the journey, they will continually learn from their own experience. The nurturing of this evolution requires risk takers or, as Joel Barker so appropriately calls them, pioneers.[1]

This is not unlike what Thomas Jefferson tried to tell us about democracy. Participatory governance is a test — something to be tried with no guarantees for success, an experiment to be undertaken with only the belief that the effort is immensely worthwhile. Judging from the current state of our nation's social problems, we desperately need to create supportive environments that encourage such risk takers.

The current national frenzy over school reform and restructuring can trace its beginnings back to the sixties, when a belief system began to resurface questioning the ability of schools to equitably benefit all children, particularly children coming from poverty and deprived conditions. This belief system implied that public schools do not really make a difference, that variances among children are more the result of their home environments than their schooling. The supposition was that schools filled with children from enriched home environments turn out academically superior students, while schools filled with children deprived of such home and community environments turn out inferior students.

These reemerging beliefs and other related factors prompted what became known as the effective schools research, conducted nationally over a period of years by such renowned educators as Ronald Edmonds, Lawrence W. Lezotte, and Wilbur Brookover.[2] The researchers' intent was to identify schools that were making a difference, schools that were beating the odds. They looked for schools filled with children from deprived home environments who were achieving at high levels.

The effective schools researchers were successful in finding schools that do indeed make a difference and in subsequently identifying the characteristics common to such schools. At least three of the characteristics they identified also provide a justification for participatory governance:

1. High levels of parental involvement and support

2. Collaborative collegial instructional planning

3. Individual school autonomy and the resulting flexibility

In addition to the effective schools research, a second major historical thrust that began in the seventies gave support to the participatory governance movement. This impetus was initiated and developed by a number of American educational foundations, notably the Kettering Foundation and the Lilly Endowment. The efforts of these foundations resulted in the development of a process for school improvement known as the IDEA process (IDEA is an acronym for Institute for the Development of Educational Activities), now more commonly referred to as site-based decision making or participatory governance.[3]

The original design of the IDEA process focused on the need for collaborative planning, the involvement of all constituencies, team building, consensus, and the belief that the individual school is the largest unit capable of improvement. This process design and its philosophical foundations, coupled with the three characteristics common to effective schools, noted previously, provide a major portion of the current research basis for participatory governance.

We feel it is important, early on, to state that neither the effective schools research nor the IDEA process model supports the notion of creating new local school bureaucracies. In fact, the creation of such entities would be contrary to all of the tested and proven research. Participatory governance teams can only find their legitimate functioning if their efforts enhance true and extensive involvement and ownership. Those involved in this process of change must see their primary charge as one of promoting greater autonomy and involvement in the decision-making process. Those who initiate change by creating new local bureaucracies that

A Note on Terminology

The phrase "participatory governance" means the transfer of authority and responsibility from those who hold power by virtue of law, contract, or organizational role to those not so empowered. Here are some examples of such transfer of power:

1. A school board of trustees creates a representative group of students, teachers, and parents who interview and make a recommendation to the board regarding the employment of a new superintendent.

2. A principal turns over the development of the master schedule to a group of teachers.

3. A school board of trustees and a superintendent give decision-making power and responsibility for the curricular/instructional school-site decision-making to a team made up of parents, teachers, students, classified staff, and building-level administrators.

involve only a few people simply add to the harm that is done to children and communities.

Unfortunately, many state legislatures grappling with school reform have added to local confusion by passing participatory governance legislation that restructures schools along the lines of representative governance, a form of governing in which the legislators themselves are so profoundly enmeshed. Often the legislation they design and pass is filled with language outlining such less significant items as voting procedures, the size of the team, and the length of terms of team members. Seldom, if ever, does the

4. A group of individuals (school site staff, parents, students, community-based agency workers, law enforcement personnel, local city council representatives, and business leaders) meet once a month for a year to define the purpose of education for their community.

Informal participatory governance, which often precedes formal participatory governance, is the practice of extending decision making without a written agreement.

Formal participatory governance indicates that the district has made a commitment to shared decision making through either board policy and/or contract language.

Site-based management is only one of the many possible forms of participatory governance. It is unique as a form of participatory governance in that the purpose is focused upon an individual school's improvement utilizing a team composed of all of the various constituencies of that particular school community. (See example 3 on page 4.)

resulting legislation deal with the philosophical justification of participatory governance or the process by which team members make logistical decisions regarding the structure of their own model. As a result, new bureaucracies — empowered by legislation to make decisions according to the old model of majority rule — have often thwarted the effectiveness of participatory governance, thereby violating the philosophical foundation upon which it is based, which is the extension of ownership to all those who are affected by decisions made on their behalf.

We cannot express too strongly our conviction — based on years of study, experience, and observation — that replacing the old bureaucratic structure with a new local one will fail to provide the authentic and broad participation required for long-lasting change and true improvement. We urge the communities of professional educators and concerned citizens to do all they can to correct this misguided trend and to make whatever efforts are necessary to prevent this approach from becoming part of their efforts to build a viable approach to reform.

To confer decision-making power upon a small number of people and call them a site council or a site-based management team reduces community involvement to an advisory status. Little is changed as others come to understand that their participation carries no more weight than it did before, and that all-inclusive community involvement in developing and carrying out a mission statement is mostly an illusion. As this realization spreads and deepens, more and more of the very people necessary to the success of the participatory governance process will abandon the effort to improve local schools. "Our schools" will once again become the responsibility of others; they will remain "their schools."

Notes

1. Joel Arthur Barker, *Paradigms: The Business of Discovering the Future* (New York: HarperBusiness, 1993). The term "pioneers" was used by Barker to describe the innovators who drive paradigm shifts.

2. "Effective Schools" is a service mark of the Institute for Development of Educational Activities, Inc., National Center of Effective Schools, as is "Effective Schools Research." The capitalized phrase denotes the comprehensive model espoused by the National Center for Effective Schools, 259 Regency Ridge, Dayton, Ohio 45459, (513) 434-6969. We use the phrase "effective schools research" with lower case letters because we mean to refer to not one specific model but to a selection of

characteristics cited by numerous researchers over the years in their various studies.

For more information about the effective schools research, see the following publications:

Wilbur Brookover, et al., *School Social Systems and Student Achievement: Schools Can Make a Difference* (New York: Praeger, 1979).

Edmonds, Ronald, "Effective Schools for the Urban Poor." *Educational Leadership* 41 (1979): 32–37.

Edmonds, Ronald, "Some Schools Work and More Can," *Social Policy* 9 (1980): 28–32.

Lezotte, Lawrence W., "Effective Schools Research and Its Implications" in *Citizen Action in Education,* Vol. IX, No. 1 (June 1982).

Lezotte, Lawrence W., "Strategic Assumptions of the Effective Schools Process" (Okemos, MI: National Center for Effective Schools, 1988).

Lezotte, Lawrence W., *Creating the Total Quality Effective School* (Okemos, MI: Effective School Products, Ltd., 1992).

Lezotte, Lawrence W., and Barbara C. Jacoby, *A Guide to the School Improvement Process Based on Effective Schools Research* (Okemos, MI: Effective School Products, Ltd., 1990).

Lezotte, Lawrence W., and Barbara C. Jacoby, *Sustainable School Reform: The District Context for School Improvement* (Okemos, MI: Effective School Products, Ltd., 1992).

3. Kettering Foundation, 200 Commons Road, Dayton, Ohio 45459, (513) 434-7300. Lilly Endowment, P.O. Box 88068, Indianapolis, IN 46208, (317) 924-5471.

ONE

The Foundation

HISTORICALLY, SCHOOLS HAVE been a reflection of the larger society of which they are a part. Who will be taught, what will be taught, and how teaching will occur have been influenced by the values and belief systems of each school's surrounding community, especially the professional educators and community leaders who are elected to develop and maintain each system of education. As social conditions have changed, schools have adapted as best they could, attempting to hold on to long-established beliefs about what schools should be. Occasionally, curricula and teaching methods have been modified in an attempt to keep pace with emerging knowledge about how learning occurs and to meet the changing needs of those served by the schools.

For a long time and for the most part, however, schools have remained essentially the same. With the participation of strong, supportive families, schools were able to produce sufficient numbers of students who could qualify for the programs of study required by the professions. The schools also produced enough workers for the factories, offices, and service industries. They taught most people what they needed to know to raise a family, to understand democracy, and to vote.

Even when challenged in the early twentieth century by large numbers of immigrants, schools were still able to transmit the core of knowledge needed for these new citizens to join in and contribute to the larger society.

Further, the situation was not entirely bleak for those whom the schools did not serve as well. For a long time and unlike today, even students who dropped out could find work.

Over the past forty years, changes have come so quickly and have been so profound that schools have found it increasingly difficult to adequately educate their students. Schools are now severely challenged; some are totally overwhelmed. There are many reasons why our schools are experiencing such a crisis.

The family was once a unit that provided a safe, nurturing environment in which most youngsters could grow and develop; they entered the schoolhouse ready to learn. The family no longer exists in that sense. Vast numbers of children now fend for themselves at home, on the streets, and on school campuses.

Advances in technology, while in some ways helpful to learning, increasingly offer serious competition for the precious time essential to learn the basics. Ask any teacher or parent and they will tell you that TV and electronic games consume hundreds of hours of time every month that children could be spending on book reading, homework assignments, or physical activity.

In addition, growing numbers of children are living in (or near) poverty. This affects city, suburban, and rural schools by weakening and, in some cases, virtually eliminating the middle class, which has been the major benefactor of public schools. Violence, drugs, physical and emotional abuse, disease, and teen pregnancy have all added to the increased burden placed on society, a burden that is inherited by schools.

We are experiencing a growing population diversity, the result of new immigrants and newly empowered native citizens. This has created a need for new teaching techniques and a knowledge about the learning styles of students who do not come from traditional backgrounds. Meeting the needs of children with disabilities is another awesome task that all school systems must face. In addition to educating for a job or for higher education, schools are pressured to take on many tasks that formerly were carefully excluded from their province.

Now it is common for schools to educate young people about the danger of drugs, how to protect themselves from violence, and the responsibilities and consequences of becoming sexually active. Schools often become agents for dispensing food, training young mothers and fathers in parenting skills, and (in some cases) providing medical and psychological advice and referrals. All of this is being done in an attempt to provide what so many families and other institutions do not (or cannot) provide.

While all of these social problems are obvious, other critical issues facing educators are not so obvious. These issues address the way schools must function if they are going to teach our children to be productive citizens and to be responsible members of society. How can schools provide children with the tools to live personally satisfying and enriching lives? To answer this question, we must reevaluate our understanding of the purpose of education.

We must examine the foundations of the educational institutions to which we have tendered the responsibility for fulfilling our educational goals. We must assess with great care what our graduates need to know and how children learn best. We must dispense with myths and invalid opinions about who can learn and what they can learn. Our basic beliefs must be questioned and our existing attitudes about some of the underpinnings of our educational system must change. In the light of the latest research and taking into consideration our own personal experiences, we need to carefully look at the issues that have influenced the way schools currently operate. We must reexamine student motivation, how we measure ability, our practices of differentiated intellectual grouping, and rigid curricula that set fixed time frames for learning.

This is an enormous task, and because of the range, complexity, and severity of the problems facing educators, we need to take a very different approach to finding solutions. We cannot do this successfully with small groups of isolated professionals and a handful of community leaders. No one group can come up with simple, one-size-fits-all answers. We cannot solve or eliminate our problems by looking back to the basics of yesterday, or by restoring discipline, or by kicking kids out of school, or by allocating

more money to schools, or by setting national standards. Some of these pro-
posals may be helpful, perhaps even necessary, but no one way is sufficient
to address the growing needs of students.

After years of commissioned research, it appears that we must look for a
new way to ask questions, develop answers, and implement solutions. For
this to occur, we need greater degrees of committed involvement, the kind
of involvement that gives ownership to the people affected and encourages
a sense of stewardship. When a whole community is involved in setting
goals and finding ways to meet those goals, the community is more inclined
to do whatever it takes to monitor progress and ensure success. To move
toward this kind of dedication, we need teachers, students, parents, administrators, school district trustees, and community members to work closely
together. We need these people, school by school, to come together to share
their knowledge and experience so that new insights can be developed.

Success will not be ensured if the approach is casual. A small number of
leaders who form an advisory group that meets occasionally over a short
period of time will not come anywhere close to finding solutions. We need
a process that enables all participants to learn as much as they can about
what works and why, so they can make informed decisions about what to
do and what not to do, about what risks to take and what risks seem unjus-
tified. We need a process that allows communities to join in making decisions about what their schools ought to be and what changes need to be
made to support continued progress toward a shared vision. We need to
embrace the process known as participatory governance.

PARTICIPATORY GOVERNANCE AIMS to meaningfully involve all
those people who are affected by decisions made relative to the educational
structure in their community. By involving and empowering widening cir-
cles of representative individuals, communities can gain the power to shape
the culture and the essence of local schools. Issues such as educational purpose, attitudes about children, curricula appropriateness, and which attri-
butes and skills are needed to live well in the twenty-first century can be
more effectively addressed. Because participatory governance brings with it

ownership, the chances of success are much greater than when a small group of individuals meets as a commission, task force, or local governing board and attempts to set an agenda for all with one curriculum, one program, and one measuring stick.

Making educational decisions through participatory governance impacts all levels of a community. To move toward such a democratic and inclusive process brings some confusion, often resentment, and always resistance as the security of old ways of thinking and functioning are challenged and altered. To engage in this process of change, participants must be willing to learn through study and the observation of communities where such processes are demonstrating success. The process of participatory governance requires building high levels of trust where formerly there was little. It is a process that requires patience, persistence, and support at the highest levels of bureaucracy and a willingness on the part of all to take risks, share power, and be accountable.

Participatory governance offers no easy answers and no quick fix. It is a mechanism to gather the best thinking about the purpose of schools and all that flows from that purpose. It provides, in a significant way, an opportunity for all members of a community to arrive at a consensus about where they want to go and what they must do to meet their educational needs. It is a powerful way to approach educational reform, allowing people to move with confidence instead of with hesitation, confusion, and fear.

For many years, bureaucratic processes were the only mechanisms used to define the direction of public education. Consequently, we have become quite astute at creating and running bureaucracies. Even so, and to our dismay, bureaucratic structures have proven to be inefficient. Far too often they are incapable of creating effective schools or fostering the kind of educational change that could result in effective schools. This becomes clearer when we review the effective schools research, which illustrates that bureaucratic organizations, as they perform their traditional roles, are generally inefficient when improvement is desirable.

Participatory governance is the direction that many school districts have now chosen as their preferred school improvement process. Since this is a profoundly different concept, it is essential to briefly define and then expand on what we mean by "participatory governance." The process includes the following components:

1. The establishment of mechanisms that allow people in a given community to arrive jointly at specific decisions or plans of actions for a particular school and then to initiate necessary changes in specified areas.

2. The involvement of all facets of a school community: parents, teachers, administrators, community representatives, and students.

3. The eventual creation of a vision or mission that reflects the best possible conditions for all students and the adults who work with them, including a safe, positive environment and appropriate opportunities to learn.

4. The establishment of extended involvement processes that will gather and disperse information and ideas in order to maintain the highest level of inclusion possible.

Participatory governance is a process with a rationale that can be conveyed to parents, teachers, students, administrators, and community representatives. The rationale includes a central tenet: People affected by decisions should have a share in making those decisions. When applied to the classroom, the most effective instructional programs or teaching techniques are those in which the people responsible for implementing these programs and using these techniques actually feel ownership and have responsibility.

Those who choose to use this process must understand that because communities are inherently unique, programs and practices in participatory governance designed by one school community are likely to differ from programs and practices designed by another school community, even within the same district. Whatever the design, all programs should move toward fulfilling the district's mission or purpose, assuming that the purpose came into being as a result of a process that involved the community. If the district mission or purpose was developed by the superintendent or by the school board or by a hand-picked "blue-ribbon" committee, then those who are charged with carrying out the mission — parents and district employees — will have little or no commitment to that purpose.

Within the confines of existing legal limitations, there is a wide arena for potential decision making. The restrictions are the same as those that applied to the former bureaucracy. They include such things as Supreme Court decisions, mandated programs, and federal and state laws that relate to educational processes. Securing waivers from existing policies or initiating legislative action is appropriate and often necessary, and this should not be misunderstood as violating legal parameters.

In establishing participatory governance, change must evolve within the existing bureaucracy. For a period of time, the educational system will be run simultaneously by two different parallel organizations: a traditional bureaucracy that is changing its power structure and the newly emerging organization of both empowered and formerly unempowered groups of people. Everyone involved needs to understand that some decisions, for a time, will continue to remain under the exclusive authority of one individual, one group, or a governing board. Thus, even though the change in power through participatory governance is an orderly process, it inevitably will create conditions of chaos.

The steps that need to be taken to implement the process of participatory governance will be discussed in later chapters. Before explaining the process further, we need to put forth the reasons why participatory governance is so effective in ushering in long-lasting change.

1. Participatory governance is better for the students.

The results of research lead us to believe that participatory governance will be a catalyst to better learning.[1] When teachers and parents are empowered to determine their mission and then design and implement their own curricula, instructional strategies, and assessment mechanisms, they will enjoy claiming ownership. This, in turn, enhances the potential for success for we work hardest at and do best with that which we own. We are also most inclined to improve what we have personally initiated, thus creating the type of "learning organizations" suggested by Peter Senge in *The Fifth Discipline.*[2]

2. Participatory governance is based on democratic principles.

The movement toward participatory governance reflects our country's commitment to the concept of democracy. Even though some people may not feel morally obligated to create an educational system that reflects democratic principles, most citizens feel that democratic principles are the primary reason for the existence of public schools.

3. Participatory governance is a part of modern political evolution.

When we look at some of the most powerful events of our time — Chinese students standing in front of tanks, the tearing down of the Berlin Wall, the demands for civil rights by minorities both here and abroad — we see people who are demanding more involvement in the decisions and circumstances that affect their lives. As in these political events, albeit on a less dramatic level, participatory governance in education is another example of a natural response to what exists in the hearts of a growing number of people: the desire to share in the events and processes that affect their lives. From this perspective, our engagement in participatory governance is not so much a benevolent initiative from the top levels of an educational institution as it is the result of a natural evolution or movement toward empowerment of all people.

4. Participatory governance accommodates changes that go against a long-standing tradition.

Participatory governance is more than a commitment to democracy; it is more than a facet of our political evolution as human beings. It is also the only way we know to abandon long-standing educational traditions. Over the past fifty years, we have seen most attempts to improve or change public education fail. When we analyze this lack of success, we frequently find that failure was due to the lack of involvement of those people who were most affected. Whenever we stray from what we might call our nation's collective understanding of public schools, this failure is most evident.

If we were to ask most people to describe what public schools mean to them, we would most likely hear about textbooks, homework, semesters, teachers, tests, schedules, grade levels, and report cards. As a result, any attempt to change these familiar features runs into trouble. For example, look at the efforts of Robert Anderson, an educational pioneer who began a movement toward nongraded schools.[3]

Despite research supportive of nongraded schools, people have become so used to grade-level designations that their elimination has consistently been met with intense resistance. Thus, efforts to eliminate grade levels, begun in the early sixties, never really took hold. This nongraded concept is again being proposed in some school reform movements, and success or failure will be tied to any given bureaucracy's ability to extend ownership.

5. Participatory governance is based on the proven fact that the largest unit for effective change is the school itself.

Additional support for participatory governance at the school-site level comes out of the research on effective schools. This research stresses that the largest unit of effective change is the individual building or school community.[4] As a matter of fact, our own observations over the past ten or fifteen years have led us to believe that effective change does not occur because of district-wide direction from the top levels of administration or because of board policy decisions. This holds even when districts are small, with four or five schools within the school district that are all deemed effective.

There are effective schools everywhere. We find them in large school districts and in small school districts. We find effective schools in every state. But the largest unit for effective *change* is the school itself. This research provides one of the strongest arguments for participatory governance at the site level.

6. Participatory governance allows educators to be creative and to take credit for their successes.

The most profound and important contributor to a successful educational program is the quality of the interaction that exists between teachers and their pupils. This quality of interaction is most enhanced when teachers are free to design and carry out their art form with the knowledge and support of their local community.

Teachers need ownership if they are to feel good about their work. People who work in an area that is more artistic than scientific need immense latitude if they are to perform well. In an area that is purely scientific, where things are precise and concretely measurable, less discretion needs to be given to the individuals performing the task. But in an area like education, where after years of debate even national commissions made up of the most prestigious members of the education profession are unable to define precisely what is meant by good teaching and effective learning, the concept of ownership is critical.

To allow people to create their own particular way of teaching seems to be of paramount importance to the educational endeavor. In communities where such ownership has been encouraged, dedicated participants have implemented many outstanding designs. In such places, citizens have endorsed innovative curricula of their own design while others have adopted the relevant features of various models.

Some empowered teachers have altered instructional time by dismissing students early one day each week so that teachers can have time to plan lessons and to meet with each other. Many empowered teachers have sought and received waivers to change grade-level definitions. Some have chosen to substitute counselors for administrators. In a few cases, dynamic risk-taking teachers have created a new school or an alternative school within the traditional school.

Philosophical Discussions Should Come First

A year or so ago, after presenting the concept of participatory governance to a group of business and industrial leaders, I was stopped in the hallway of the convention center by a CEO who wanted to compliment me on my conference remarks. He was particularly pleased by my mention of the need to eliminate the sorting and selecting system in which many school communities are engaged. He advised me that two years earlier he and his top administrators had attended a four-day conference conducted by Ed Deming, the quality management sage.

At this particular conference, as described by this CEO, Deming had expressed the critical need for American educators to cease their current grading practices because they were destroying the children being sorted to the bottom. Deming maintained that the grading system was contributing in a significant way to the growing number of young people either dropping out of school or finishing so ill-prepared that they were unable to find even entry level work.

As the CEO walked away, a second conference participant standing nearby while we talked approached and introduced himself as the superintendent of a local school district. With half a smile on his face,

continued on page 20

continued from page 19

he stated that he could not help overhearing my conversation with the CEO and asked if we could sit and talk somewhere over coffee. I agreed and he shared with me the following story.

The year before a number of teachers and administrators, representing several schools in his district, decided to institute cooperative learning groups and portfolio assessments in an effort to move away from the sorting and selecting process based on the competitive grading system. No parents were present at either the training sessions that led to the desire for change or at the meetings where the details of the change were planned and scheduled.

Shortly after these changes were initiated, this superintendent was contacted by two members of his school board. He was asked to meet with a recently formed group of rather influential parents (some were local CEOs) who were quite upset about these new practices. Their concern was that their children were college bound and their grades were part of the assessment mechanism used to determine potential scholarships as well as entry into preferred colleges.

The superintendent was baffled. He and his staff had already met with these parents, carefully articulating the philosophy behind the new approaches. The parents acknowledged that they understood — clearly understood — but they wanted the schools to figure out how to do this without adversely impacting their children.

The superintendent concluded his story by telling me that he would spare me the details of the next six months of political hell in his district. He confided that if his board had not been so supportive throughout the whole ordeal, he might have considered a job change.

I cannot envision a system more difficult to alter than one whose flaws, weaknesses, obstacles, and deficiencies have extensive ownership from one segment of the community they serve at the expense of other segments of that same community. If any kind of change or improvement is to take place, the people who are going to be affected by those changes must be involved. Community members must be included in philosophical discussions; this will promote an understanding of the need for any changes prior to initiating them. Otherwise, the result will be something like what this superintendent described to me. Everybody suffered — school trustees, administrators, teachers, parents, students — *and* educationally sound practices were reversed because those affected by the change did not understand either the importance or the significance of the change.

— RJG

ANY SCHOOL DISTRICT that begins a serious consideration of participatory governance needs to deal with a number of predictable issues, especially mind-sets that have developed over many decades of traditional approaches to education. The issues surrounding these mind-sets must be clarified so that the level of discomfort felt by the many persons involved in this change process is kept to a manageable level.[5]

The Power Mind-Set

Several years ago I received a phone call from a building principal who advised me that he and his staff had made a major modification in the delivery of services to special education students. He invited me to come to his building, for he and his staff were anxious to show me what they had done. I will never forget walking down the hallway of his building while he enthusiastically shared with me details about the change that was underway.

When we reached the special education area of the building, it was obvious that what was offered to these students and their parent volunteers was an educational design filled with ownership and based on an enthusiasm that ensured success. Yet even as I stood there, marveling at what had been accomplished, my gut reaction was that my authority had been usurped, that I should have been contacted *before* the changes had taken place. I cognitively understood that power is significantly greater when shared, yet inside I continued to carry the vestiges of my former understanding of how schools should be and my almost primitive feeling about power and the territorial imperative.

We inhaled this need for power and control in our youth and, as adults, we have exhaled it onto the next generation. Every day for the rest of our lives, we must consciously learn to breathe anew.

The Win-Lose Mind-Set

During a recent meeting with a group of high school students, we got into a discussion about the real meaning of grades. To illustrate my feeling about grades, I turned to a young man in the first row and asked him, "What grade would you like to receive in this course?"

He glanced over at his teacher, smiled, and said, "An A, of course."

"What if you got the A and you were sitting at your desk, looking at your final exam — a big, red letter A in the upper right corner? How would you feel?"

"Great," he exclaimed.

"Now you turn to your neighbor — you can see his paper. It has on it a large red A+. You turn the other way and see a student with an A++. Behind you is another A++." I paused. "Now how would you feel?"

"Not so good," he quickly replied. "I'd wonder what I did wrong."

Inside all of us is a clear understanding, as we've been taught, that the world is filled with winners and losers. A win-win philosophy is essentially foreign to us. For the most part, one student's A is based on the fact that another student received a D. It's not that the teacher wants some students to get D's, but in this system everyone clearly understands early on that we all can't be winners.

Or can we?

The win-lose mind-set is deep and powerful and, like the power mind-set, it has an emotional as well as cognitive impact. Turning away from the win-lose mind-set gives a whole new meaning to grades, but it is even more significant than that. Most participatory governance models require some eventual movement toward consensus and involvement of divergent groups of constituents in arriving at that consensus.

If we follow the win-lose mind-set, as we have been taught, in restructuring our schools some parents (those who think grades are important, for example) lose and others (those who feel more learning takes place without the competition inherent in the win-lose mind-set) win. With the win-win mind-set, out of confrontation we can hope for a negotiated settlement where each side claims victory. Although essential to the successful implementation of participatory governance, collaboration and win-win run counter to the win-lose mind-set that we learned in early childhood and have most likely practiced ever since.

The Problem-Solving Mind-Set

Most participatory governance models train participants to go back to their sites and collectively create a vision of improvement, answering the question, "What is the best education system that you can imagine?" This collective vision creation is powerful, for it transcends the natural inclination to use problem-solving as the mechanism for change.

Deep within all of us is a feeling that improvement or change must somehow be directed to perceived problem areas. Further, each of us has little personal experience of effective change through vision creation. Our natural inclination is to define a problem, gain support from those who think as we do, fashion a solution to the problem, and lobby to get the majority vote for our position. We leave those who have lost in our wake, and in many cases they now prepare to act in a way to ensure that our solution will fail.

The Model Program Mind-Set

Some years ago, one of my sons came to me and said, "Dad, I'd like to build a desk for my room." Delighted, I enthusiastically shared with him some of my thoughts on how the construction of his desk should take place. As I now recall, he patiently listened to me and, as I was nearing the end of my detailed explanation, said politely, "Dad, if you don't mind, there's another way I'd like to do this."

Having more than a passing knowledge of carpentry, I advised him that there *were* various ways of constructing a desk, and I was confident that what I had shared with him was one of the better approaches. He again patiently responded, "Dad, really, if you don't mind, let me try my way."

As God had blessed him with a perceptive mother, I was tactfully persuaded to let him do it his way. For the next three days, I watched my son fashion a creation that consumed him to the point of missing meals and his customary amount of sleep. In the end he completed his desk — nothing that I would have highlighted in my living room, but a desk that he would not trade for the most fashionable desk in the most expensive furniture store. It was uniquely functional and, best of all, he enjoyed sitting at his desk and working on his studies. At times I could even see him take a study break, feel a corner, smile, and know that he had made it and sanded it the way he wanted it done.

There is something magnificent about ownership — doing something the way we feel it should best be done. Yet in education, we persist with the mind-set that someone else's way, tried and tested, is the best way: the model program. This mind-set permeates the entire institution to the point where only our strongest and most secure teachers feel comfortable deviating.

Our district offices are filled with individuals skilled at securing money from various organizations (including state departments of public instruction) as long as this money is used for programs that follow prescribed designs. Many of these programs fail to exist beyond the original funding period, for they engender little or no ownership on the part of those who have to implement them.

What is produced and owned by a school community will be cherished, nurtured, and improved if necessary. It may not be the pedagogical ideal, but it will meet the needs of the affected children.

The That's-Reality Mind-Set

Several years ago, students identified by the district as promising young leaders were invited to spend an all-expenses-paid weekend at Notre Dame University, participating in a youth leadership training program. One year there were two students whose names were very similar — John P. Williams and John T. Williams. John T. was a member of the National Honor Society and had an oustanding curricular and extra-curricular record during his first two years of high school. John P., on the other hand, was categorically defined as learning disabled. Although he attended school regularly, he did not excel academically and never participated in extra-curricular activities.

Through a clerical error, John P. Williams received the written invitation to the leadership program, and he decided to attend. (The error was not noticed until after the students returned from the program.) Several weeks later, the building principal complimented his staff, particularly on the selection of John Williams. He had been advised by Notre Dame that John showed the leadership qualities that those conducting the workshop truly admired. I am confident that John P. Williams responded at Notre Dame according to his understanding of their collective perception of what they thought he was. In fact, they created a new reality for John P.

If those involved in the participatory governance process are expected to create visions of an ideal reality, then we must somehow enable them to clearly understand that reality *can* be fashioned and changed. Reality is in large measure what we collectively believe it to be, particularly as we act in accordance with that new belief.

IT IS IMPORTANT to remember that the participatory governance process carries no guarantee that effective schools will be the final result. However, we have seen this process work in many different locations and in districts with many different characteristics. We have found participatory governance to be a most worthwhile undertaking.

Participatory governance is a process that every school needs to examine carefully before attempting. It cannot be forced upon a community or a school. To do so is a misunderstanding of the intent, and the result is usually failure. Each school community should decide whether or not to make a commitment to participatory governance. Should not the first act of a democracy be to allow the people to decide whether or not they wish to be democratic?

Notes

1. See footnote number 2 in the Introduction, page 6.

2. Peter M. Senge, *Fifth Discipline: Mastering the Five Practices of the Learning Organization* (New York: Doubleday, 1990).

3. Robert H. Anderson and Barbara Nelson Pavan, *Nongradedness: Helping It to Happen* (Lancaster, PA: Technomic Publishers, 1993).

4. R. Edmonds and J. Frederickson, "Search for Effective Schools: The Identification and Analysis of City Schools That Are Instructionally Effective for Poor Children," ERIC Document Reproduction Services No. ED 170 396.

5. The description of the five mind-sets (pages 21–26) was previously published in "School-Based Management Pitfalls: How to Avoid Some and Deal with Others," by Raymond J. Golarz (*The School Community Journal,* Spring–Summer 1992, Vol. 2, No. 1, pages 38–52). An earlier version of the same material appeared in *Handbook on School-Based Management: Restructuring Schools for Excellence through Teacher Empowerment,* edited by James Lewis, Jr. (Westbury, NY: J. L. Wilkerson Publishing Company/National Center to Save Our Schools, 1991, pages 102–108). Grateful acknowledgment to both of these sources for their kind permission to adapt this material.

TWO

The Cornerstone

THE PARTICIPATORY PROCESS should begin with a definition of the purpose of education (a mission statement) and with an examination of the social issues that will shape the curriculum. Indeed, given the widely diverse attitudes regarding the role of education in our society, it is in the best interest of all concerned if the participatory process starts by defining the purpose of education.

The first principle of quality management is continuity of purpose. Though quite common in business, a precise definition regarding what a school is trying to accomplish has been largely ignored in education. Since ongoing mandates stipulate what must be taught, defining the purpose of education can seem to be an exercise in futility. Year after year, vested interest groups have succeeded in getting their state legislatures to mandate their view of what should be added to the curriculum. In addition, every year new pressures are put upon schools to carry social burdens that are the result of disintegrating families and other formerly strong institutions.

The coordinated efforts of concerned citizens, educators, parents, and all other affected members of a community are needed to improve our schools. No one should be overlooked — not the bus driver, not the custodian, not the local business owners, and surely not the students. No longer can groups of people work in isolation, at cross purposes, or without the necessary understanding and support of those who are affected by their

An Inclusionary Process

I recently visited a rather progressive school district in Arkansas. I had been asked to assist in the development of an evolving participatory effort, including a redefinition of the district purpose. As I was working in one of the schools, one of the teachers told me that her students were quite distressed because their bus driver was retiring. She had repeatedly tried to get her students to accept the driver's retirement, but felt she had failed. She asked me if I would talk to the children. I agreed and asked her to tell me all she knew about the bus driver.

"I know his name is Mike," she told me, "and that he appears to be quite kind. However, he usually has trouble getting his bus loaded on time after school."

My talk with the children was brief. All they could do was express their distress at losing Mike and they asked me to make him stay "'cause he's our friend."

With only one thing left to do, I went looking for Mike, who turned out to be a very pleasant-looking man in his mid-sixties. I apol-

decisions. All of the issues surrounding the role of public education — issues that relate fundamentally and consistently to the purpose of education — must be addressed: funding, assessment, curricula, values, standards, teaching strategies, the allocation of resources, and the hiring of personnel.

In *The Best Kept Secret to Achieving Successful School Management,* Carol Grosse, a superintendent in Phoenix, and her colleague, Terri Fields, describe how educational goals are often determined by a few individuals and known by only a handful.[1] Little is done to foster involvement in defining the school's purpose, and even less is done to allow people in the organization to know how they can contribute to making the goals a reality.

ogized for intruding into his business and assured him that I was not trying to dissuade him from retirement. "I am interested only in knowing why the children, in your opinion, hold you in such high regard," I told him directly.

Mike said that about three years earlier he had overheard the principal tell the teachers that a corporate purpose had been adopted. Mike described this purpose as the need to get the kids to believe in themselves and be proud of their accomplishments. Mike had been on his route for a long time and knew that most of his kids went home to an empty house. He also told me he noticed that the kids often left their school papers on the bus, even the ones with stars and smiley faces. He concluded they had no one to share the papers with when they got home. Keeping the new purpose in mind, Mike began asking the kids, as they entered the bus, to show him the papers that made them proud.

"Do you think I did the right thing?" he asked me. "It does take longer to load the bus."

— *RJG*

To begin the process of participatory governance, each community needs to carefully examine any existing definitions of the purpose of schools and then update them with an eye toward what children will need to survive and thrive as they enter their adult years. To do this effectively, the questions of the "what" and "who" of public education must be answered:

What should we teach?

Who should be educated, and to what extent?

After answering the general questions, specific questions need to be answered: Should our primary focus be on producing students who can read, write, and do mathematical calculations, leaving all other areas of development up to the family? Should the schools be teaching values? If so, which values? Are we obligated to offer instruction in the arts, athletics, social skills, and citizenship? Should we focus on the college-bound student? Or should we focus on job preparation, allowing business to set our goals and curriculum content? Finally, and possibly most importantly, after we define the "what" and "who," are there processes to ensure that each person in the organization knows how he or she can contribute to making the purpose become a reality?

Defining the Purpose of Education

If you were to walk into many communities in America and ask in an emotional tone, "What do you think we really need to do with our schools?" some people, regardless of their educational level, would suggest that our schools should return to reading, writing, and arithmetic, taught in a well-disciplined environment. We believe that many resort to the more traditional view of the purpose of public education because our current perspectives cannot envision the types of schools that are needed now.

Most of the current information available to us regarding the purpose of education significantly differs from this simplistic back-to-basics view. For example, the U.S. Department of Labor's SCANS (Secretary's Commission on Achieving Necessary Skills) report, "What Work Requires of Schools," which came out in 1991, identified the skills children need now and will need in the future.[2] The report does not negate basic skills training, but does go well beyond the traditional reading, writing, and arithmetic skills of the past. Notably included are interpersonal skills — the ability to work with others, to participate as a member of a team, and to contribute to group effort. Other skills noted relate to thinking skills — the ability to work creatively, make decisions, solve problems, visualize, learn how to learn and how to reason. The personal qualities of self-esteem, responsibility, sociability, and self-management are also mentioned.

Another significant 1991 report, this one from the Center for Workforce Preparation and Quality Education, conducted by The Roper Organization from New York, also points out the need to go beyond the traditional skills.[3] This report identifies skills necessary currently and for the future: good work habits (again noting the need to work with others) and, echoing the SCANS report, the ability to deal with the public or the consumer in an appropriate manner. Also identified were reasoning skills and the ability to work with minimum supervision. Both the SCANS report and the report from the Center for Workforce Preparation and Quality Education include reading, math, and writing as necessary skills, but these skills are no longer viewed as the only critical or necessary goal of public education.

Many communities are incorporating interpersonal and critical thinking skills in their curricula. In some places, professionals are joined by parents and other community members in an effort to identify such skills. One example of such an effort can be found in Richmond, Indiana. Through the guidance and assistance of Dr. Phillip Harris, director of the Center for Professional Development and Services of Phi Delta Kappa in Bloomington, Indiana, a process was developed to clarify the purpose of public education. A survey was sent out to the entire community. Nearly two thousand people completed the survey over a period of approximately fifteen months. These people represented a cross section of Americans — they were rich, poor, black, white, young, old. They listed thinking and reasoning skills as number one for high school students. Second were the traditional skills of reading, writing, and mathematics followed by conflict resolution or the ability to come to agreement. The same survey asked these community members to identify the values they believe students should learn in school. They felt respect for one's self (self-esteem) was the most important value to learn.

These are not isolated examples. American public education is moving toward a more clearly articulated definition of the basic skills necessary for a productive and satisfying life, which include the three R's coupled with other skills related to inter- and intrapersonal functioning. This conclusion corresponds to the plethora of articles on education that recommend more emphasis on nonacademic (or living) skills in current curricula.[4] This is an

A Lack of Clarity

Some years ago I was invited to Arizona to address a group of teachers and administrators regarding the concept of restructuring. The day before my scheduled speech, I had the opportunity to visit several local elementary schools. While walking through the hallway of one elementary school, I came upon a teacher who had brought two young boys out into the hallway. She was explaining to them not only why they should not fight, but why they needed to get along. The two children, first graders, were crying — the fight had obviously just ended. The teacher was down on one knee, gently attempting to get the boys to understand her message. The teacher noticed me standing there, observing her and the boys.

The next morning as I stood in front of the group, I noticed that teacher in the audience. Later she came up to me and we talked for a while about restructuring in general. She then explained to me that I had found her in the hallway the day before because she felt compelled to deal with the fighting problem even though she was supposed to be teaching math at the time. She was somewhat apologetic and seemed concerned that I might have made a negative judgment

interesting trend because it reverses the movement of the sixties and seventies, a period of time when schools backed away from the very areas that people now regard as essential.

Just because there appears to be such harmony regarding educational purpose, do not conclude that we can set aside the issue and establish national or state standards and goals. This is a short-sighted idea, as evidenced by the long history of state and national governing agencies either directly setting standards or exerting a powerful influence over such standards without success. Such history of failure exists and will predictably about her lack of focus on the basic skills that she was supposed to be teaching.

In one sense, fighting has always been dealt with by classroom teachers, though usually in terms of disciplinary action. As a manifestation of a breach of good conduct, fighting is action that schools do not tolerate, largely because it is a disruption of the educational process. In this instance, however, the teacher was not imposing punishment nor sending the children to the principal's office. She was trying, instead, to get the children to understand why people have to get along and she considered this message important enough to take time away from an instructional activity.

I often reflect on this particular experience because I think it illustrates the lack of clarity that we have in our schools regarding the purpose of education. If that purpose is not specifically articulated, then even veteran teachers can become confused regarding the activities they should be structuring for children on a daily or hourly basis. That veteran teacher in Arizona is not unlike so many of us in both the American and international communities who believe that the primary purpose of public education continues to be only the teaching of basic skills.

— RJG

continue as long as definitions come from the top, ignoring the need for more representative involvement and precluding potential ownership of those who are charged with carrying out the mission.

We seem to possess a national mind-set that those who hold political power and/or perform their roles at the upper levels of bureaucracy are somehow mystically empowered to make wiser decisions. What if we could set aside this mind-set and endorse for a moment the belief that virtually any group of people can arrive at wise decisions when they are provided with the same information that so habitually is provided to persons in authority? Of course, this concept does threaten the very existence of bureaucracies and hierarchies.

The only edge that bureaucrats hold over the rest of the people is access to information. If all that is known at the upper levels of government or educational organizations were shared, then decisions at all levels would be made more wisely. In addition and most importantly, the directions chosen by those most affected would include ownership and a commitment to making things happen. As David Clark and Terry Astuto so capably point out when discussing McGregor's motivation Theory Y, in their article "Redirecting Reform":

> . . . people will exercise self-direction and self-control in the service of objectives to which they are committed; that commitment to objectives is a function of the rewards associated with their [own] achievement. . . .[5]

Who most appropriately defines the purpose of education? Our history as a nation reveals past definitions of purpose that were quite articulate and well thought out for their times but suffered erosion over the years primarily because they did not have the understanding or extended ownership of either parents or educators. Most of the old definitions were fashioned by leaders without the involvement of constituencies.

Participatory governance is founded on the belief that the people who define the purpose of education, if the intent is for general support and extended ownership, should be those at the local level who are most affected by and charged with carrying out the purpose. This means that key individuals representing all the constituencies of the school community need to have meaningful input into the process and be in accord with the final product.

A small group of professionals cannot sustain an educational purpose that contradicts the view held by the larger community. Unless the entire community is involved in defining the purpose of education, within a very short time the principal and teachers will be required to change their activities to conform to the perception that the community holds for the purpose of public education. For this reason, as part of the participatory governance process educators need to schedule meetings and have extensive discussions with various groups of people throughout the community. These discussions must involve the multiple constituencies of the community and focus upon the "what" and "who" questions: What should be taught? Who should be educated, and to what extent? Only this kind of intensive dialogue can give clarity and ownership to a community's chosen direction.

Many school districts have tried an alternate process called strategic planning. This particular process relies upon the efforts of a special committee of people usually selected by the school board and/or the superintendent. These people, often as many as a hundred, are asked to define the purpose of schools for their district. In addition to the definition, they also are asked to outline the activities that will be performed school-by-school in order to comply with the definition they have formulated. Although much better than the school trustees going off on a retreat to define the purpose of education in total isolation, this particular strategy still falls short of the kind of involvement we are advocating. The result is little ownership by the full community.

If participatory governance is to succeed, extensive efforts must be made to involve virtually every member of the community affected by the schools. Once this is understood and embraced, then the process can be developed by the community. In fact, allowing everyone to have a part in defining the purpose of education will begin group engagement. The end result should be a clear definition of purpose that everyone can support.

Community groups usually come up with as many as eight or more elements that represent the kinds of proficiencies or skills they want children to have. Indeed, many communities have incorporated much of what is in the SCANS report, especially if given access to current information about what children need to know to become productive members of our rapidly changing society. The input of current information is critical. To ask people to define the purpose of education without directing them to appropriate resources is irresponsible and ineffective. Part of the rationale for participatory governance is the recognition that the people who are closest to

A Plaque for the Gateway to Education

We recently visited Ohio University in Athens, Ohio. There, on a gateway structure marking the entrance to the campus, we read these words:

Religion, Morality, and Knowledge
Being Necessary to Good Government
and the Happiness of Mankind,
Schools and the Means of Education,
Shall Forever Be Encouraged.
                    Ordinance of 1807

Some person or group of people had defined the purpose of educa-

children, especially parents and teachers, will define the purpose of education as wisely as a school board or a superintendent — *if given the same information.*

Be careful not to leap into participatory governance by saying to all who will listen, "Go forth and create your purpose." Rather, begin by sharing information and encouraging intensive dialogue regarding the purpose of education. This is especially necessary if the community at large is being asked to support the latest educational trends. For example, many teachers are turning toward cooperative learning, but before implementing this new method, they should inform and engage the community. Which old methods are being thrown out when cooperative learning takes over as a primary mechanism by which children will learn? What happens to individual effort? How are individual assessments made? A foundation must be laid before change begins. Success depends on the support of all involved in the process.

tion. In 1807 the definition may even have represented the opinion of most citizens regarding the purpose of schools.

As individuals, we may still endorse all or parts of this statement.

As a nation, however, over time we have determined some fundamental changes from the philosophy presented here. These changes have not perfectly or definitively resolved all the issues nor answered all the questions that continue to be raised regarding the purpose of schools. It seems imperative, therefore, that citizens continue to debate these issues and attempt to answer the questions — new and old. Do we agree today that good government and the happiness of mankind are still important and that education is the key to obtaining them? In the late twentieth century, what will we write on the gateway marking the entrance to an ideal school? In the late twentieth century, who will decide what will be written and how will this decision be made?

Before setting out to define your educational purpose, you also need to know that your community may come up with a purpose that differs from what the majority of citizens in this country see as the ideal. Even if this is the case, people must be allowed to choose their own path — as long as they stay within legal parameters. For example, a community may decide not to teach values; some people prefer that activities related to how people get along with one another not be part of the educational process. Even though we can see the importance of such value teaching, we would still allow that particular community to choose its own direction.

Change, any change, has practical and philosophical implications. If we look at the last thirty or forty years of public education, we see many attempts at educational change with few lasting results. This does not mean that the change itself was wrong or unnecessary, only that the change confronted some deeply held beliefs and the outcome of the change was not sufficiently convincing.

Valid questions are continuously asked about how children are being taught to read, do math, and understand language. A number of innovative teaching techniques have been introduced, yet few have been incorporated into the core curriculum. In the sixties and seventies, people were figuratively and literally storming the schools, demanding educational change. In the name of educational reform, curricula were labeled as outdated, middle class, racist, and irrelevant. Demands were made for profound changes to better reflect respect for the individual, women, and multicultural diversity. As education systems attempted to respond to these demands, a messy patchwork was created that often did not have a clear direction or definition. We wanted to improve education, but we did not understand how to create sustained change.

Now we have a much clearer understanding that if we are going to have sustained change, we have to use processes that involve all those who have a vested interest in the outcome. This means that the institution of education, unlike IBM or Inland Steel, cannot create significant change within its organizational structure unless all constituencies are heard from and agree that the change is necessary. This again explains why participatory governance must be all-inclusive.

As Scott Peck suggests in *A World Waiting to Be Born,* people charged with making decisions or plans for change or improvement must come together.[6] In the process of participatory governance, people must interface in new ways so they can create a mission that is clearly representative of the needs of *all* children in our diverse communities.

Accommodating Varying Learning Potentials

Americans believe in equality. The story of our development as a nation is replete with efforts to make this belief a reality. Long, bitter fights have occurred throughout our history as we have tried to live up to this ideal.

Slavery, voting rights, property rights, and discrimination of all kinds and at all levels have been at issue. The way we educate our children is of particular significance in this context. Since its beginnings, the concept of public education has embraced, at least intellectually, the notion that all children have an equal right to an education. That we have not always delivered in an equitable fashion is an obvious and grievous failing. This failing has consumed the energy of our schools and courts, indeed our entire society, for at least forty years. Much has been done to resolve the discriminatory acts that have segregated children according to race. However, erroneous notions about innate intellectual ability still exist, notions used to justify a system of education that sorts and selects, often on the basis of faulty observation and unsophisticated or inaccurate testing.

The wrongs brought by this faulty sorting system have been further compounded by the perceived need to rigidly organize our educational system. The prescribed use of defined and outlined curricula has precluded valid alternatives. For many educators, this means a lost opportunity to teach children in such a way that they can overcome disabilities or disadvantages.

For most of our educational history, the idea that all children can learn has carried with it certain qualifications. This is evident when we look at the way children are labeled, a system of compartmentalization that greatly affects how educational opportunities are funded. The categories into which most children are placed run along a continuum from gifted at one end to disabled or high risk at the other. While the original intent of such compartmentalization might have been to help children reach their highest potential, this approach has to a significant and often tragic degree precluded this from happening.

Any community seeking to define its educational purpose must examine how it views children as learners. What does it mean to say "all children can learn," a statement that many school systems routinely include in their set of beliefs? Any community involved in the effort to provide appropriate educational experiences for *all* its children must reevaluate the concept of intellectual ability as well as the funding that occurs as a result of how the concept is understood. Failure to do so will ensure continued inequity.

We need to acknowledge that the institutionalization of such inequality exists throughout our schools and is tied in great part to some very deeply held beliefs. These beliefs, founded in the erroneous scientific research done by a number of universities in the early part of the twentieth century, promoted the notion of differentiated levels of intellectual abilities based upon ethnic and racial origins. Even today we have researchers attempting to promote such erroneous theories. The research suggests the existence of a general intelligence factor computable for individuals which, when grouped, shows a normal distribution along a bell-shaped curve. Imbued in these erroneous concepts, teachers, administrators, and educated citizens have created schools that reflect such thinking. A full explanation of this topic is in Stephen Gould's masterful work, *The Mismeasure of Man*.[7]

From assumptions based on the inappropriate application of the bell-shaped intelligence curve and other misconceptions about intellectual ability, a curriculum has evolved that arbitrarily creates tracks within our schools. Primarily focused upon mathematics and language arts, this curriculum is quite rich for students who are perceived as having superior abilities. For the student with so-called "average" ability, less demanding or differently geared subject matter is selected. Some of the students are guided to remedial basics and vocational education.

Unfortunately, vocational education is often inadequate because schools find it too expensive to keep up with the rapid changes in technology, both in terms of the necessary equipment and the professional development of the teachers. This dramatically weakens the schools' ability to prepare their students for skilled vocational jobs. In addition, since these students represent the lower end of the bell-shaped intelligence curve, a greatly watered-down curriculum gives them minimal instruction in reading, writing, and mathematics. Their curriculum focuses on either remediation or the most basic of life-skills courses. The future for these students is grim. They are likely to find employment only in low-paying, zero-benefit jobs that offer little opportunity for advancement. They receive neither an equal nor an adequate education.

What is increasingly apparent is that today's students must be able to think mathematically and critically, engage in deductive and inductive reasoning, and get along with coworkers. These skills are required by everyone. We are not suggesting the need for a core curriculum. Each of us learns from our own vantage point. Where one student may find mathematics to be a genesis point, a second student may find music or art to be an avenue to desired knowledge. What we are suggesting is that all students should have access to a demanding and diverse curriculum, a course of study that may include the old basics but that is enhanced in key areas to meet society's rapidly changing needs.

Such a curriculum might well incorporate elements emanating from the new and expanded definitions of intelligence as proposed by Harvard's Howard Gardner in his classic work, *Frames of Mind*.[8] According to Gardner, an expanded curriculum adds elements such as interpersonal skills, body kinesthetics, and music. Now in operation at Key School in Indianapolis, this has been shown to provide opportunities to students who have been excluded in the former, less diverse curriculum to become successful in broader areas.[9]

In determining educational purpose, other out-dated and erroneous mind-sets must be addressed because they affect scores of young people, often in devastating ways. First we need to look at the assumption that the child who learns quickly is the only child who can be called "gifted." We assume that the child's power to learn at an accelerated pace implies a better quality of learning. Conversely, children who do not learn as rapidly are perceived as less "bright" and able to learn only from a slower rate of presentation or a less demanding content.

This has a profound significance in our society. *When we believe that mental quickness is a prime indicator of intelligence, children are misplaced — often as early as the first grade.* This error may be perpetuated throughout a child's school career and bring with it frustration and failure, which in turn can lead to discipline problems, damaged self-esteem, lost hopes, and (for many) an early exit from school. This practice continues despite the knowledge that significant numbers of students have demonstrated that when they are able to

Time As a Variable

After graduating from high school, I decided to go to college. I had no clue what I wanted to study, but engineering sounded fascinating. I chose Purdue University and signed up for seventeen credits the first semester of my freshman year: chemistry for engineers and scientists, analytical geometry, calculus, and on and on like that.

The second week I said to myself, "This isn't going to work." I significantly lightened the load by eliminating the chemistry for engineers and scientists. I vividly recall the professor for that course, a man who could write on the board with his right hand while simultaneously erasing with his left. I wasn't really upset at the brief exposure to his creativity because I didn't know what he was putting up there anyway. My concern came from observations of my classmates who, to a person, expressed frustration that he was going too slow. My seventeen-year-old mind said, "Ray, these are not your people, but perchance that they are, they have been digesting something that isn't yet on your menu."

At the end of the first semester I ended up with a 5.6 grade point average (on a 6-point scale). When friends and acquaintances said, "Ray, you're brilliant," I always responded the same way: "You don't know how smart I am — I'm not even sure I'm a full-time student anymore."

Some years and many adjustments later, I graduated with honors. And the most profound commentary is that over the years since I graduated, no one — truly no one — has ever asked me how long it took. I learned something of lifelong value in finishing at that slower pace: The pace doesn't matter. Time can and must be a variable. Further, I understood firsthand that all of the architecture that makes up formal education must be revisited to see if it fits the students served or if the students have to be forced to fit the architecture.

— RJG

control the amount of information, the combination of courses attempted, and the rate at which they progress, they can succeed and achieve at the high levels necessary to enter into demanding professions and careers.

Most teachers are well aware of the capacity of most students to experience success when curriculum design can be adjusted. However, the structure of most schools continues to adhere to a curriculum that requires students to proceed in lockstep. The educators who supported the idea of grouping or tracking did not intend to cause harm to young people. Rather, they wanted to make the American system of education available to all children. This system ascribed to the belief that the main purpose of education was to teach children to learn *to the best of their ability* and that grouping by ability level would accelerate the process. The rationale was that slower children would not be as frustrated and brighter children would not become bored.

In actuality, those children labeled "slower" fall even further behind and those children perceived as "brighter" often become isolated from the main body of students and lose the opportunity to acquire necessary skills. Some of these children who are labeled "bright" in the early elementary grades are unable to maintain the same level of effort. Though they may be fast learners in elementary school, a few of these brighter children are actually less adept at acquiring certain kinds of knowledge, especially when analytical or critical thinking are required, or when special creativity is the basis of a lesson.

As long as we continue to firmly believe in the normal distribution of the variable called intelligence and in the speed of learning as the prime indication of intelligence, our schools will continue to employ sort-and-select mechanisms. Fortunately, many teachers now see the faulty premise on which these assumptions are based. Two highly publicized teachers have refused to believe in the accuracy of such sorting and selecting.

Marva Collins, founder of the West Side Chicago Preparatory School, is one teacher who truly believes in the potential of all children to learn.[10] Her school is founded on the belief that when they are given time, effort, caring, and appropriate strategies, children who had been labeled unable or unwilling to learn can indeed learn, often at exceptionally high levels. Another teacher, Jaime Escalante, featured in the movie *Stand and Deliver,* also proved that when children are personally respected, provided with the necessary instruction and support, and challenged with something even as difficult as calculus, they will achieve far beyond anyone's expectations.[11]

Why have these two teachers, as well as many others, experienced success when others have failed? Most likely it is because their beliefs about the ability to learn digress very significantly from the way the traditional education system usually deals with children. These two outstanding teachers refuse to lower their expectations. They do not limit their time to the established school clock. They seek to develop intimacy and trust with their students. They understand that children respond to people who believe in them. They understand and practice what outstanding learning requires. And they employ teaching styles that foster what they believe.

One final and major consequence of accentuating intellectual differences is its impact on funding. In *Savage Inequities,* Jonathan Kozol describes the disparity that exists in terms of the education funding base.[12] He suggests that the source of the savage inequities in education is often the result of tax-base variations. Communities where the tax base is exceptionally low are at a severe disadvantage because the resources available to them are minimal compared to other, more prosperous communities. This is certainly true.

However, the savage inequities *within* any high school in the country, public or private, make Kozol's suggestion of the differences between districts pale by comparison. The gifted programs and the special education programs, including those for high-risk students, receive more money per student than the programs for mainstream students. In most districts, this dollar disparity exists.

For example, let's examine a typical school system, where the expenditure per student is $4000 per year. We can readily see an expenditure differential if we compare the yearly expenditure on an advanced placement, college-bound student taking chemistry, physics, advanced math, and a foreign language with the yearly expenditure on an "average" student in the same school taking general math and general English. The expenditure gap widens if we figure in the differences in class size and the cost of extracurricular activities, which generally draw more top-level students than average or remedial students.

Our intent is not to suggest that all children can learn all subjects equally well at all times. However, communities need to reevaluate how learning potential and curriculum design can be restructured to enhance the learning potential of all students. We must look closely at which skills are deemed necessary and at who will identify these skills.

We already see pressure coming from different facets of our communities as parents and others are beginning to challenge how the education system services children. As the business and industrial sectors increase pressure, we will see a heavier emphasis on basic job preparation. In fact, many fear that preparation for the workplace may supplant the need to provide students with a well-rounded education that will teach them how to be responsible citizens in a democratic society.

While we ponder the impact of special interest groups, we also need to decide which curriculum will be appropriate for all students and how that curriculum should be taught. A core curriculum focusing on information that is memorized and regurgitated on command will not prepare students for the world to come. We must instead provide students with generic skills that permit flexibility and the freedom to move in any number of directions, skills such as how to learn, how to think through a complex problem, and how to interact with an unfamiliar group of new people. The ability to work successfully with others, no matter how different, is becoming increasingly necessary for everyone.

It seems overwhelmingly clear that in addressing the issue of who is to be educated in this country, we must reevaluate these critical beliefs and practices:

1. The mind-set that only a small percentage of students are able to succeed at high levels.

2. The rigid standardization of curriculum that focuses primarily on the acquisition of information.

3. The adherence to rigid and arbitrary time frames for the learner.

Finally, educational reformers must never lose sight of the fact that there is a crucial need for all students to acquire the thinking and interpersonal skills that will allow them to function in a world that is changing dramatically and at an increasingly accelerated rate.

Notes

1. Carol Grosse and Terri Fields, *The Best Kept Secret to Achieving Successful School Management* (Phoenix: Innovative Materials, 1986). Copies of this book can be ordered directly from Innovative Materials, 3142 E. Rose Lane, Phoenix, AZ 85016. Send $10 plus $1.50 for postage and handling.

2. United States Department of Labor, Secretary's Commission on Achieving Necessary Skills (SCANS), "What Work Requires of Schools: A SCANS Report for America 2000" (Washington, D.C.: 1991).

3. "Public Education: Meeting the Needs of Small Business," (New York: The Roper Organization, Inc., 1991). This report was conducted for the Center for Workforce Preparation and Quality Education, an affiliate of the United States Chamber of Commerce.

4. See footnote number 2 in the Introduction, page 6.

5. David L. Clark and Terry A. Astuto, "Redirecting Reform," *Phi Delta Kappan* 75 (March 1994): 515.

6. M. Scott Peck, *A World Waiting to Be Born: Civility Rediscovered* (New York: Bantam, 1993).

7. Stephen Jay Gould, *The Mismeasure of Man* (New York: W. W. Norton, 1981).

8. Howard Gardner, *Frames of Mind: The Theory of Multiple Intelligence* (New York: Basic Books, 1985).

9. Tina Blythe and Howard Gardner, "A School for All Intelligences," *Educational Leadership* (April 1990), 33–37. The Key School Option Program is at #97, Indianapolis Public Schools, 1401 East Tenth Street, Indianapolis, Indiana 46201.

10. Marva Collins and Civia Tamarkin, *Marva Collins' Way* (New York: St. Martin's Press, 1982).

11. Jay Mathews, *Escalante: The Best Teacher in America* (New York: Henry Holt and Company, 1988). Ramon Menendez's 1988 movie *Stand and Deliver* (now available as a Feature videocassette) is based on this book.

12. Jonathan Kozol, *Savage Inequities: Children in America's Schools* (New York: HarperCollins, 1991).

THREE

The Building Blocks

SEVERAL ELEMENTS COMPRISE the essential building blocks for participatory governance, and these elements can be sequenced to ensure success. Here we'll leave the philosophical basis and look instead at five very practical aspects of participatory governance: community involvement, team building, pyramiding, visioning, and consensus.

Community Involvement

As its name implies, participatory governance requires the participation of many people. All groups that make up a school community must be involved: teachers, parents, administrators, noncertified staff, community representatives, and students. Involving other members of the community is a challenging task. Failure to do so may sow the seeds for future problems. Community support and ownership of new school improvement plans is crucial for meaningful and long-lasting change.

Community involvement can be achieved in many ways:

1. Access to parents is built in for many schools because many parents are already involved as members of parent-teacher organizations and as volunteers in the schools. These parents are extremely helpful in recruiting other parents to become actively involved.

2. Teachers and administrators at the site can actively pursue parents. Since broad representation is the goal, the superintendent, the principal, and classroom teachers can approach parents who rarely become involved, telling them that their participation is earnestly needed and that they will find this unique experience an opportunity to improve their child's education. All avenues of communication should be used, including letters, messages in the school newsletter, and a well-coordinated telephone tree.

3. An effort must be made to communicate with the wider community. Sometimes information can be presented in conjunction with other routine meetings, including parent-teacher association meetings and school board meetings. Presentations on local television stations and coverage in the press are also productive ways to convey the message that something special is going on and that community involvement is welcome.

4. The effort to increase involvement and invite participation can be explained at an initial informational meeting.

Time is an important component. The scheduling of meetings is always problematic — no time is ever satisfactory for everyone. Creativity and flexibility help. While working with an urban, inner-city school whose staff had complained "We can't get parents to come," Dr. Gary Phillips asked the students when they felt their parents would feel most comfortable meeting with staff members of the school. The students told Dr. Phillips that such a meeting would have the greatest potential for success if the meeting took place on a Sunday afternoon at the community center, away from the school building. Only eight to ten parents had ever shown up for a meeting, but several hundred came to the community center on the scheduled Sunday afternoon.[1]

Parents tend to feel uncomfortable in their dealings with school officials. Their relationship with school personnel is often limited to evaluation conferences or special conferences called because of problems their children are having. These situations, awkward at best, can be very intimidating for parents.

Parents need to feel comfortable at any participatory governance meeting. It is especially helpful if all meetings, from informational beginnings to organized team meetings, are held in a setting where parents are treated as equals and where, from the outset, they feel they really are a crucial part of a movement toward general improvement for all. Actually, such a gathering at someone's home creates an especially welcoming atmosphere.

Many schools have found that such meetings are positively received when combined with a simple dinner, perhaps a potluck. This provides an opportunity for professional staff, community representatives, and parents to meet and talk on an informal basis before any organized agenda is considered.

Let parents know that even if they do not want to become part of the team their general support and their willingness to be part of a feedback structure would be a vital contribution. Whatever form of communication is used, parents need to understand that they are not just being asked to join an advisory committee, that their involvement is sought in a dynamic effort to make educational improvements.

If a school draws students from several disparate communities, school officials must take special steps to insure parental representation from all neighborhoods, particularly if the communities are racially, socially, or culturally different or identifiable. To suggest that this is not possible because some neighborhoods lack leadership is simply false or (more kindly put) terribly naive.

The same approach should be used to engage members of the community who may not have school-age children. Contact local businesses and social organizations such as the Chamber of Commerce, the Lions Club, and the Kiwanis Club. Foundations should be contacted and asked to send representatives to meetings. Many communities have higher institutions of learning, extensions of their state universities, or vocational schools. These institutions are keenly interested in the public schools and are very willing to send representatives from their teaching or administrative staffs. They also can contact their population of students, who are often very eager to participate.

Contact with all these citizens usually produces a surprisingly large number of people who are willing to actively participate in this process. Others will offer support in smaller but significant ways, especially if they feel their contributions will be viewed as important and likely to have a real impact on the schools.

Participants need to understand from the outset that their function will not be to replace teachers, administrators, or board members. Rather, they will have a voice in shaping the purpose of their schools, in creating a vision for their schools, and in designing ways in which the vision can become a reality. Thus, their roles are collegial and in no way less important than the jobs of the professional staff. If participatory governance is to work, this is a promise that the school system must never violate.

Team Building

Community involvement is on-going and gives credence to the participatory governance process. However, large groups are logistically limited and a site-based action team, a mini-representation of the larger group, must be designated. Ideally it works best if the selected individuals are facilitator types who are interested in promoting processes and not personal agendas.

One of the most difficult steps that a school district will take is determining the composition of the site-based participatory governance team. A worst case scenario is to have the team members picked by the school principal. If that is done, the team is likely to be perceived as controlled by the administration. It will appear to be another top-down structure because the principal is seen by most people as part of the bureaucratic hierarchy. Even though this is not a simple task, it is better to have teachers pick teachers and parents pick parents.

Experience dictates that the best composition for a participatory governance team is one that strikes a balance between school personnel and people who are not employees of the school system (parents, students, senior citizens, members of the business community, social agency personnel, and those who are active in local political and service organizations). Building principals and others who are helping to form a team should always remember that numbers alone cannot guarantee adequate representation for any constituency. For example, having seven or eight teachers on the team is not as important as having seven or eight teachers who best represent the faculty. Those who are forming the team must ask each constituency to select people who truly represent that group's diversity in terms of thinking, ethnic origin, race, formal educational level, profession and/or teaching area.

Teams seem to function best when equal numbers of parents and teachers account for the major portion of the team. This offsets the possibility of domination by any one sub-group. Student representation always adds a healthy dimension. Teams of twenty to twenty-five members seem to function best for the task of site-based management. With fewer people than this you rarely achieve appropriate representation. In large schools, notably high schools, it is possible to have more than one site-based team, particularly when faculty, parents, and students are interested in creating schools within the school.

Once the selection process is completed, the primary task is to turn this group of people into a cohesive team. The critical importance of this task has been sorely underestimated by many who have undertaken the process of participatory governance. Most of these newly formed groups try to bypass the team-building process and move immediately to the formation of a plan. They ignore the necessity of allotting time to allow the newly formed group of diverse individuals to willingly set aside their own personal agendas in the interest of group progress and group goals.

Evidence of the omission of this step can be seen when some group members let others control and dominate the agenda and the dialogue. Feeling powerless, these team members often resort to making private contact with those they see as having power in the traditional school bureaucracy (school board members, administrators, officers of the parent-teachers association, and leaders of the teachers' association). While silent during the meetings, these team members are very vocal in their complaints about the state of affairs on their new site-based team. They call for help. They complain that the process will not work.

These individuals are victims of poor team building. An essential step has been overlooked, so these individuals reach out beyond the group, often without advising fellow team members of their personal distress. Those who receive such complaints should not respond by using their bureaucratic position to take sides or place blame. Team members who express such distress must be directed back to the group itself. The newly formed group is by design a diversity of people and this very fact demands that significant communication occur. Unless group members know one another, including how their opinions differ, they will not be able to function as a team in any meaningful sense.

As with the initial community-wide meetings, it is helpful to gather the people together in places that are removed from the school. If by necessity the meetings are held at school, choose a time that is not during the normal school day.

The process of participatory governance is now at the stage where many people who do not know each other meet in a room. All want to see improvement but few know each other. Here is where team building must begin — at the first meeting. Customarily, it is beneficial to begin with what are called human development activities. These activities should go beyond the usual self-introduction and engage the team members in exercises that call for them to explore attitudes and exchange opinions about issues in a nonthreatening manner.

Brainstorming, with its built-in mechanism that encourages people to make suggestions without criticism, is an effective way to allow all members to contribute to the discussion. Selecting a topic (for example, describe your favorite teacher) helps people focus on elements that relate to school in a positive manner. Such an exercise will provide the basis for an interesting interchange as people begin to share some of the feelings they have about how schools operate.

A brainstorming session like this also might lead into an exercise in arriving at consensus. In this case, the task might be to make a list of the characteristics a good teacher must have. Such a task would reveal the many different perceptions people have regarding many issues surrounding effective education.

Since these teams will be charged with many tasks, organizational as well as substantive, some time must be spent presenting information. Guidelines for the processes involved, parameters for the team's involvement, information relative to effective schools research, careful descriptions of how to further involve the school community — all need to be part of the agenda of these meetings during the start-up phase. But it is truly critical that the members of the team come to trust and respect each other in a very meaningful way. If team members are going to accommodate differences and still come together in a process to make their school more effective, then they all need to understand the things that have shaped individual attitudes.

As teachers, administrators, students, parents, and community members talk about how they feel about schools, it quickly becomes obvious that many people have had painful and frustrating educational experiences. The primary purpose of these meetings should not be to provide an opportunity to settle old grudges or reveal complaints about particular people. This would be unethical and counterproductive. These meetings are not gripe sessions or arenas for gossip, but rather a place where people from all backgrounds can share their concerns in a nonthreatening and nonblaming manner. This is the way to provide a meaningful foundation upon which a collective vision can be built.

In this previsioning stage, the team members should think about and discuss a host of practical and philosophical questions:

What makes it difficult for teachers to teach?

What gets in the way of students feeling comfortable enough to learn?

What do parents fear when they send their children off to school?

A Teacher's Lament

I can recall a day some years ago when Marion came home quite late and obviously very depressed. She wanted to go out to dinner for she needed to talk. I agreed and we went to one of our favorite restaurants.

At the time Marion was a teacher at the secondary level. After we were seated and ordered our dinner, she told me the problem: "I need to talk to you about my fourth period class." Beginning with the first student she described all of the things that she knew about his childhood — the abuse, neglect, protective service involvement, and foster home care. Then she explained what she was attempting to do for this student on a daily basis.

Next she told me about a second student, who was as needy — if not more needy — than the first. And again she explained what she was attempting to do during class in order to help this child. Then I heard story number three, story number four, and so on until there was a total of twelve such stories. When she finished she asked, "What do you think?"

Somewhat overwhelmed, I recall saying, "I really don't know what to say."

"You see, Ray," she told me, "I don't have just twelve students in that class — I have thirty — but the immense needs of those twelve absorb all of my time and I can virtually never get to the other eigh-

All over the country, both teachers and parents are experiencing tremendous frustration. As these feelings are shared within the context of the team meetings, visions of improvement will come forth. It is critical to get these sentiments out in the open, so when the time comes to make decisions all opinions are considered. The answers to these questions should direct the vision that is ultimately created and how it is implemented.

teen. And the really sad thing about all of this is that I am not sure that I'm doing anything of real significance with the twelve I'm spending all my time with." She concluded with what has become an all-too-familiar phrase in education: "I don't know how much longer I can do this."

My wife cared deeply about those students. Nearly every teacher cares deeply for the students, but there are conditions under which teaching is almost impossible, conditions that make the anticipated product of teaching not happen in the way the teacher had hoped. Most often these are conditions out of a teacher's control: the experiences children have had, the backgrounds they come from, and the social conditions under which they must function.

The parent who is sitting on the participatory governance team needs to hear this kind of story from the teacher who is often blamed for a child's inability to learn. Teachers, too, need to hear about the real pain and frustration that parents experience with an equal sense of hopelessness. Like teachers, parents have stories of overwhelmingly difficult conditions and of feelings of inadequacy, of not knowing where to go or whom to turn to for help with some of the problems their children are experiencing. Finally, both teachers and parents, as well as other members of the team, need to hear the stories that students have to tell. Surely they have insights for everyone who hopes to improve schools.

— *RJG*

People who are sitting on participatory governance teams need to get past their own personal frustrations. They need to stop looking for enemies and for people to blame. If you are to succeed, you need to convince those who are active participants in school reform that we are all less than perfect human beings facing overwhelming problems. The group needs to try its best to change the conditions that lead to such frustration.

Team building is of immense importance. If members don't understand each other's frustrations, they will not have the strength or cohesion to deal with really complex issues as a group. Many opportunities should be afforded to share stories such as "A Teacher's Lament" (see pages 58–59). As the stories unfold, group members will see what is important and what is truly valued. After people are allowed to share their feelings, discussions will easily follow that illuminate the real issues. Even if such stories reveal attitudes and values that stir up disagreement, there is great value in getting to know where people stand on important educational issues.

Given time and the freedom to be honest and open, the members of a team will be better able to fulfill their charge of making their school the best it can be. This will not happen quickly or painlessly. Frustrations and suspicions do not disappear overnight, and deeply held convictions do not immediately change just because they are out in the open. Differences and disagreements all have to be worked through, and this can be difficult and time consuming. However, unless these feelings and opinions are out in the open, there is little hope for the kind of thinking and cooperation that will allow teams to really move forward.

Sometimes a professional facilitator can be asked to attend team meetings. If no trained facilitators are available locally, facilitation training can be provided to those who are interested in the group process. A number of national training organizations offer this kind of assistance.[2] It is imperative that the group receive whatever assistance members need to move them to higher levels of interpersonal sensitivity and establish the processes that will ensure everyone's involvement in an equitable way.

There are many sources for help. Other communities that have engaged in such training can offer suggestions and sometimes provide trained personnel. Most businesses and universities have engaged in this type of training or have knowledge about where to go to get information on appropriate assistance. Sometimes team members go off on a weekend retreat to try to coalesce as a team. This "state of community" can be illusive and does not occur because people spend a weekend together. Many opportunities must be provided over a sufficient period of time for people to overcome their own barriers and build trust so they can focus on helping their community design and implement educational improvements.

The Pyramid Process

The pyramid process is a very efficient way to extend involvement and ownership beyond the site-based team. Although the pyramid process does not fully involve everyone in the school community, it is relatively simple and helps the team involve more people. In the pyramid process, each person who is a member of the participatory governance team agrees to interact with three or four other people not on the team who have a vested interest in the school community.

The pyramid process, as illustrated in the figure on page 62, greatly increases the number of people who are involved in participatory governance. These people are routinely contacted between meetings. The members of the site-based team should consider the members of their pyramid structure to be a valuable resource for gathering additional information and as a source of feedback about the topics that are being discussed during the team meetings.

A typical conversation with a member of the pyramid structure might begin like this: "Damon, last week you agreed to be a member of the pyramid structure. I wanted to let you know that at our first meeting we discussed nongraded schools, portfolio assessment, and report card modifications. Do you think these issues are worth pursuing? Do you have any strong opinions about any of them?"

Beginning with the second meeting of the participatory governance team, the very first item on each agenda should be pyramid structure reports. If the process is followed faithfully, any plan developed by the team will never come as a surprise to the school community.

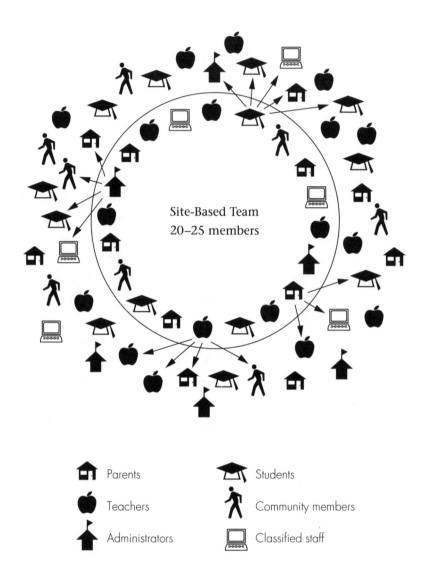

Parents

Teachers

Administrators

Students

Community members

Classified staff

The Pyramid Process

Every member of the site-based team interrelates with three or four people of their own choosing. As a result, close to a hundred people are peripherally involved. Some coordination needs to occur so team members are not pyramiding with the same people.

Unfortunately, within six months many teams stop using the pyramid process. Even when they are well-trained, team members often act like the apostles in the Garden of Gethsemani — fully intending to stay awake but falling asleep anyway. This is not to say that any group intentionally ignores such a valuable process. Team members need to know and remember that participatory governance is committed to involving additional people rather than having team members make decisions on their own. Perhaps some team members will find it too difficult or too time-consuming to relate to several people in this new mode. All team members need to know that this is a critical activity, one that needs to be developed and used on an on-going basis.

A few other guidelines should be kept in mind regarding the pyramiding process:

- While the idea is to involve as many people as possible, team members should not engage more people than they can comfortably maintain. The aim is to stay in contact with a few individuals over a long enough time period to get quality feedback.

- Team members need to relate to their pyramid contacts in a way that genuinely solicits their opinions. Information received about how other people in the community perceive the team's actions or contemplated plans is invaluable.

- Information from pyramid contacts, especially when negative, needs to be conveyed to the team as completely as possible. These messages should not be modified or edited.

- Team members need to guard against telling their pyramid process contacts "what we are doing" as though decisions have already been made. This defeats the purpose of the pyramid process since people would then question whether their opinion will really have a significant impact.

Creating a Vision

After a representative team has been formed, essential team building has taken place, and a pyramid structure established, the next task is the creation of a school vision. When a group of people gather to improve an organization or a condition within an organization, they normally and quite naturally assume their solution lies in problem solving. The process model we are describing and recommending moves away from this problem-solving approach for very important reasons. People often cannot agree on what the problems are, what causes the problems, or which problems need to be solved first. Even if agreement on these issues can be reached, the solutions are often superficial because they address symptoms and not causes. In addition, the problems have a tendency to resurface as soon as the pressure is off. This frequently happens when those given the major responsibility for initiating the solutions become involved in other new procedures or more pressing issues.

There are other conditions that occur when we attempt to bring about effective improvement by addressing specific problems. This approach frequently involves trying to find out who or what is to blame, which is not productive. We can rarely point to one enemy or one set of conditions and say, "This is why we have a problem." This problem-solving approach can also create extreme resentment and resistance as some people feel unfairly blamed or unfairly burdened by proposed solutions.

Finally, the problem-solving approach does not work because most people do not understand that whatever measures are taken to solve problems within a system as complex as a school system will have an impact on other parts of the system. Sometimes the impact is mild. More often it is significant, and not infrequently it is profoundly disturbing. This impact is increasingly felt as the changes made to solve a problem begin to affect those who have adjusted in order to function under adverse circumstances.

Seven or eight years ago, a new principal was hired in a Midwestern inner-city high school. His story will illustrate the complexity of change and the limited effectiveness of attempting to fix a specific problem in an isolated fashion. Without consulting his professional staff, he took steps (in concurrence with a perception held by some members of the community) to solve a major problem facing his school — the large number of students, perhaps as many as 200, who were hanging around the hallways during class time. He hired some security officers who, at his direction, forced students to vacate the hallways. Some students went to their classrooms. Most went home. The hallways were cleared.

To this principal's dismay, his teachers were extremely angry. The veteran faculty called an emergency meeting. They informed the principal that his actions had created an impossible situation. The teachers told him that they, too, were keenly aware of the many students loitering in the hallways. However, he needed to understand that the problem had not developed overnight. For many years the teachers had attempted to convince their administrators that the 1910 building needed to be renovated.

The extremely small classrooms did not meet the state requirements for the number of students they now served. Desks were in such short supply that some students were forced to sit on the floor. Because there were no fire exits in the hallway, teachers had been ordered to keep their classroom doors closed. On warm days, the temperature in the poorly ventilated rooms quickly reached 100 degrees. Finally, as the number of students increased and daily attendance became sporadic, it was very difficult to know which students actually belonged in a particular classroom. Under these circumstances, the teachers were unable to insist that the students report to their respective classes.

The teachers did agree with the principal that something needed to be done, but they made it clear that simply clearing the halls in this manner was not going to bring about significant teaching and learning. The principal found himself in an extremely awkward position. His action had been taken partly in response to angry parents and community members. What could he now say to them? He knew their attitude would be, "We don't care what the teachers have to deal with, we want those hallways cleared." He feared they would neither care about nor understand the concerns of the teachers regarding the educational drawbacks of the building. They could clearly see that the security officers had relieved a disorderly situation. How could he convey to his community the price that is paid when teachers are unable to teach and students are unable to learn?

After the confrontation with the teachers, the principal went to his supervisors at the central office and explained what he was up against. He had to be able to take steps to alleviate the overcrowding and to improve the facilities. The central office administrator listened patiently and then responded: "We can promise you nothing. We know all about these conditions, but you need to understand some things. First, there is not enough money to repair or improve your building. Not only is it expensive to make repairs or improvements such as enlarging classrooms or installing fire doors, we are also required, when renovating any part of a building, to bring the whole building up to code. We cannot afford to do this. The building fund is tied directly to taxes assessed on property in the community. Tax dollars are severely depleted for several reasons. Many people have moved to the suburbs, causing property values to decline. Many of the businesses that paid taxes have moved. To attract new businesses that would provide desperately needed jobs, the government has guaranteed tax breaks to new businesses, so many of these people live in a tax-free zone. We don't have the money to repair leaky roofs, much less install fire doors or enlarge classrooms. Go back and tell your staff that unless they can figure out a way to raise an enormous amount of money, they'll have to live with conditions the way they are or figure out some other solution. We can't help you now and we don't know when we can. If it's any consolation, there are at least twenty-three other schools in this part of the city dealing with the same conditions."

What appeared to this principal to be a reasonable, necessary, and relatively simple solution to a vexing problem was in reality not simple at all. The solution chosen had an adverse and troublesome impact. Students and teachers, with no warning, went from a difficult situation to an intolerable one. The new principal found himself confronted by an angry staff and a frustrated community, with no help to be found from a money-strapped central office.

Before long the security officers were let go. The hallways again became crowded with students. For a while teachers and administrators made an extra effort to get students to class. By November, when the cooler weather no longer made the closed-door classrooms intolerable, the only visible problem was evidenced by the few students in each classroom sitting on the floor. Everyone was back to doing the best they could under the circumstances, until the weather warmed up again in the spring.

Interestingly, we can relate another story about a similar school where a specific problem was "fixed" as a result of the visioning endeavor of the site-based team. This school was also a Midwestern, inner-city high school. By the early eighties, this school had developed the kind of conditions we associate with the worst picture of American public education. The attendance percentage had declined to less than 70 percent, though this was difficult to accurately measure because of the 1600 students who were enrolled only 1200 or so put in a full day. Others came and left at will. Academic achievement had declined dramatically and the buildings were covered with graffiti. Bathrooms within the building were reported unsafe; some were locked so that the limited supervisory staff could maintain some measure of control. Racial tension was high. The school had hired security officers to supervise the parking lot during the school day because of extensive vandalism and theft.

Finally, one day the worst of all things happened: The campus supervisors and the teachers lost control of the students. Hundreds of students poured out of the building and into the streets. The police were called, not only from that community but also from neighboring communities. The unrest spread from the campus into the surrounding area. For several hours, no one had control of the situation. Students wandered throughout the building and onto the adjoining streets. Some were carrying handguns, clubs, and other weapons. After control was restored, it took several weeks for the teachers and the surrounding community to acknowledge that the loss of control was not a result of suspected outsiders; rather, the conditions and environment within the school and school community were to blame.

In this kind of a crisis situation, the typical approach is a concerted effort to identify problem areas and the intensive strategies needed for resolution. Instead, these teachers — with a newly hired principal who was perceived as a very strong leader — chose to use a visionary approach to create a new school. Even though it sounded risky and they didn't know much about the visionary process, they took a leap of faith.

They formed a participatory governance team with extensive representation from all aspects of the community. The representatives included gang leaders, clergy from local churches, staff members from the legal aid society, officials from the mayor's office, new and veteran teachers, building administrators, central office personnel, and students. Together they developed a view of a new school that was, in part, the creation of those who formerly had been alienated.

About a year after this new vision had been implemented, the security officers informed the building level administrators that the parking lot was no longer a problem. Virtually no incidents of vandalism or theft were occurring. This was very significant since the problem of the parking lot had never been specifically addressed by the participatory governance team. Up until this point, the administration had operated only on faith that a visioning process, appropriately carried out, would ultimately cause systemic change. Now, for the first time, there was tangible evidence that systemic change was occurring.

So intrigued was the administration that they decided to trace the changed variables within the school that had impacted the parking lot problem. The subsequent investigation showed that those who were causing the vandalism had been coming from study halls in the school itself. Because so many students were now taking more academic subjects, there were fewer study halls. The students assigned to study hall were now using the study period for its intended purpose.

Prior to this time, study halls frequently had as many as sixty students supervised by one teacher. Attendance was not easily monitored and it was not unusual for many students to be missing for legitimate reasons. They could be absent for the day, visiting the nurse's office or the guidance department, going to the bathroom or to the library. The teachers who were in charge saw their primary obligation as maintaining order for those students who did report. Attendance was somebody else's problem. A set of interacting conditions had clearly contributed to the problems in the parking lot. As these conditions or variables were changed or eliminated, the problems in the parking lot were also eliminated.

The vision had attempted to address the concerns of all individuals at the site and in the community. Some logistical measures to monitor student movement during the day were enacted. More appropriate counseling helped students select more challenging and satisfying classes. Staff development was provided and opportunities for collegial planning were built into the schedule. Parental involvement was actively sought.

Both of these stories illustrate how difficult it is to correct or improve a system because all the variables within the system interrelate with one another. When one imperfection in a system is corrected, something or someone else will be impacted, and not always in a positive manner. As long as schools persist in attempting to create significant improvement by making a list of things that must be fixed, they will continue to be bogged down with isolated and superficial solutions that fail to address the underlying causes of the problem.

One of the most serious disadvantages of the fix-the-problem approach is the nonproductive finger-pointing that usually disintegrates into a review of old grievances. Seldom is the result any new solutions that gain support from the community. This kind of thinking is likely to be limited, negative, and alienating the very people who need to be involved.

What does it mean when a school has poor discipline, low attendance, a high drop-out rate, disproportionate numbers of failing students and/or disengaged students, low teacher morale, harried administrators, overwhelmed counselors, a high rate of vandalism, racial tension, constant fighting among students, little or no involvement in extra-curricular activities, and little or no parent involvement? As educators, how should we address these issues? Should we make yet another list of problems and respond with more rules and punishments? Should we blame our school's problems on a rotten society? On TV? On rap music? On bad teachers? Should we say nothing can be done?

Ultimately, the problem-solving approach fails to create the positive attitudes that precede change or improvement, in part because of the reasons previously noted and also, we suspect, because the efforts employed to resolve the problems are often lacking in originality and require significant additional responsibilities for those who are already overwhelmed. For improvement to occur, an atmosphere or a climate is needed that will allow — indeed encourage — all the members of an improvement team to cooperate in designing a vision that will inspire people to do whatever is necessary for those in their school to be the best they can be.

In this approach, teams are asked to look at their school environment and culture, and then envision what they would like the school to be. There are no limits outside of legal prescriptions and administrative policy. In this context, however, we need to remind the reader of one critical constraint. Any team's vision must not conflict with the district mission or purpose. Finally, the team needs to do what is necessary to ensure that their whole school community is dynamic, growing, caring, and responsive. In order to achieve this, all those involved must be as free as possible of anger, fear of failure, and free of the blame-fixing that often accompanies the old problem-solving model.

Unfortunately, some schools are so beset by severe problems that they cannot function. No design for significant improvement can occur when there is massive disorder or an absence of leadership, or when everyone's energies are devoted to putting out fires. All schools have some problems that need to be resolved immediately. Day-to-day fire control is not best addressed by a site-based team, even though such problems are symptomatic of deeper issues that should be addressed by the team.

The members of the participatory governance team are there to get something done, to give hope, to create a vision. No specific recipe is offered because just as each school's problems are unique, the vision of a new school lies within that school's community. Each school community will have a different vision, but the processes used to create and implement that vision will be the same. In visioning you will work backward — that is, you will come together as a team, aware of specific problems, but rather than trying to fix them one at a time, you will generate a picture of what makes a school work. Research, travel, observation, study, exploration, risk taking — all these are necessary components leading to the creation of a vision.

What makes a school an inviting, invigorating, engaging place?

What do teachers, students, professional and nonprofessional staff need to sustain high achievement?

What can parents or civic leaders or business people or senior citizens do to make their schools and their community a better place in which to live?

Do parents want to be given the opportunity to come to the school to learn how to help their children?

What do the members of the pyramid structure want to see happen? Do they want twenty national scholarship winners? Do they want an outstanding fine arts program? Do they want to find ways to encourage all school and community members to join together in projects that can provide much-needed service?

How can teachers be helped to overcome their feelings of frustration, isolation, and helplessness?

These are the kinds of questions, the kinds of issues, the kinds of possibilities that participatory governance and their communities must ponder.

Out of this focused team effort will come a design, a plan, a vision — the first step to a better way. If authentic, if truly developed by the whole community, the mood will begin to swing. People will explore ways to implement and refine the changes as needed. Some problems will not immediately go away. Some individuals will continue to point out the faults, open old wounds, and question pie-in-the-sky ideas. But if the effort is sustained and supported, the problems will lessen and become less disruptive as the vision becomes more real. Under circumstances that ensure open dialogue, that are enhanced by access to the latest information and research, and that are reinforced by willingness to risk or challenge ineffectiveness, teams with broad-based community involvement will create innovative visions that have the promise to profoundly affect the entire school system.

Consensus

We have already stressed the need for members of the team to become aware and tolerant of the needs, attitudes, and concerns of each other. This is necessary if teams are going to be able to make changes, for eventually the members must arrive at consensus regarding its most important functions. Consensus, an integral part of participatory governance, is the collective acceptance of a final judgment arrived at by the group. Ownership and support by all is essential. Differences of opinion must be treated as a way of gathering additional information, clarifying issues, and forcing the group to seek better alternatives.

Consensus is generally viewed as something that almost never occurs within a group of people unless they are in an atmosphere where they can be honest with each other and where the issues upon which they are working hold virtually no emotional value for anyone. Our experiences show this to be an unfounded generalization, and one too often used as an argument by those who fear consensus will work against them. To avoid the creation of an enemy in the team's own camp, which typically happens when a group makes decisions by majority vote, consensus is essential.

Another misperception of consensus is that everyone will eventually come to agreement and then be excited about and committed to what has been agreed upon. In reality, most people have different views about virtually everything. Consequently, before a group can make a commitment to consensus, the members must develop a practical definition of what consensus means. What level of agreement is necessary to consider that consensus has been reached?

Moving away from winners and losers is imperative. If nine people are in favor and five are against, the resulting condition is a divided camp. As a result, the group has sown the seed for its own demise. Those who vote against an issue or a plan or any kind of action are, at a minimum, going to do nothing to support the effort. It is even more likely that there will be active resistance.

The team should strive to avoid this by moving slowly and patiently toward consensus on one issue before moving on to the next issue. This is a time-consuming but necessary process which, if not undertaken, could lead to the collapse of participatory governance.

Each team must determine its own consensus parameters before attempts are made to act on any issues or plans of action. The team must decide what kind of support will be needed for those who are in disagreement before allowing the group to move forward.

Consensus needs to be determined building by building, not by district. If five people in a team of twenty-five do not agree with a particular way of proceeding, must the group continue to look for alternatives or compromises? What if two of the twenty-five are reluctant to support an effort? Once the numbers are decided, there's more: Which issues require consensus? Can some issues be decided by a designated person?

Of course, all of these issues need to be discussed within the context of the group. Such a simple question as "Where should the team meet?" might seem inconsequential, but under certain circumstances, it might be a very significant issue. Any action that will require significant change for any team member or for the community must be carefully debated until the understood and agreed-upon level of consensus is reached.

Many groups have successfully built an agreed-upon definition of consensus that meets the needs, style, and dynamics of their unique situation. A practical definition of *consensus* for participatory governance is that the team must come to a level of agreement whereby those in the group who are least supportive are at a minimum willing to allow that which is agreed upon by others to take place or be attempted. In *A World Waiting to Be Born*, Scott Peck describes a group's experience with the consensus process. The following definition of consensus was arrived at by a group of physicians:

> *Consensus is a group decision (which some members may not feel is the best decision, but which they can all live with, support, and commit themselves not to undermine), arrived at without voting, through a process whereby the issues are fully aired, all members feel they have been adequately heard, in which everyone has equal power and responsibility, and different degrees of influence by virtue of individual stubbornness or charisma are avoided so that all are satisfied with the process. The process requires the members to be emotionally present and engaged, frank in a loving, mutually respectful manner, sensitive to each other; to be selfless, dispassionate, and capable of emptying themselves, and possessing a paradoxical awareness of the preciousness of both people and time (including knowing when the solution is satisfactory, and that it is time to stop and not reopen the discussion until such time as the group determines a need for revision).*[3]

We stress that the individuals who make up the team must have experiences in consensus building or be introduced to the concept early in the team-building phase. All members need to be familiar with how consensus works. The team must actively support the consensus process before using it for any significant act of decision making. Failure to do this early in the team-building process will result in frustration and confusion. Sometimes it will generate strong negative feelings that can stand in the way of progress.

The effort to involve the whole community in a meaningful way must be vigorous, well planned, and extensive. Those who decide to become involved with such an effort must be prepared to make a substantial gift of time. As well, they will need a willingness to take risks, to remain open, and to be sensitive to the needs and perceptions of their diverse community constituency. No complete prescriptions can be offered, no perfect answers guaranteed, but those who become involved in this process will find it an exciting and rewarding experience. They will come to understand why participatory governance, when it is truly a community effort, is essential to effective educational reform.

Notes

1. This story came from Dr. Gary Phillips during a workshop presentation.

2. National Training Associates offers individual consultation and group training in team building, consensus building, and many other subjects related to participatory governance and school reform. Call (800) 624-1120 for more information.

3. M. Scott Peck, *A World Waiting to Be Born: Civility Rediscovered* (New York: Bantam, 1993), pp. 290–91.

FOUR

Construction Underway

WE ARE OFTEN asked what initial steps need to be taken by a school district in order to successfully implement a formalized movement toward participatory governance. We suggest the following five steps for such an implementation process.

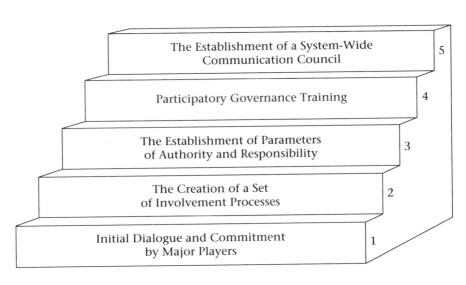

Implementation Steps to Participatory Governance

STEP ONE
Initial Dialogue and Commitment by Major Players

Fairly extensive dialogue needs to occur among the major players who hold traditional positions of power in the existing bureaucracy. Include at least the elected school board trustees, the superintendent, and the presidents of bargaining groups that represent the teachers and the noncertified staff. The group should also include representatives from other groups — students, parents, businesses, service agencies, and elected governing bodies. Often these latter groups are not initially involved because the trustees, the superintendent, and the association leadership first need some time to feel their way with one another. Each organization will dialogue in ways that are locally appropriate and in accord with board policies.

At these initial meetings, candor is very important. Those holding traditional bureaucratic positions must understand that a formalized movement to participatory governance will impact their own organizational power. The evolution of change undertaken will eventually result in more decision making power and responsibility for individual school communities and less formalized power for the school board, the superintendent, the central office, and the teachers association leadership. In fact *as participatory governance unfolds, no group or individual holding formal or informal power in the former bureaucracy will maintain the same level of power or influence under participatory governance.* Individuals in the organization formerly very powerful and influential because of their position in the hierarchy or because of their long tenure and credibility will lose some influence. Gaining in power, influence, and responsibility will be the newly formed participatory governance teams. This shift of power is illustrated on page 79.

After all major players have a clear understanding of the implications of participatory governance, they must be willing to make a commitment to the proposed evolution. This commitment must be substantial. The attitude behind the commitment cannot be "Well, we'll try it, but if it doesn't work. . . ." Such a statement represents no commitment at all. Any school district whose power players are only at the "yes but" stage should not ven-

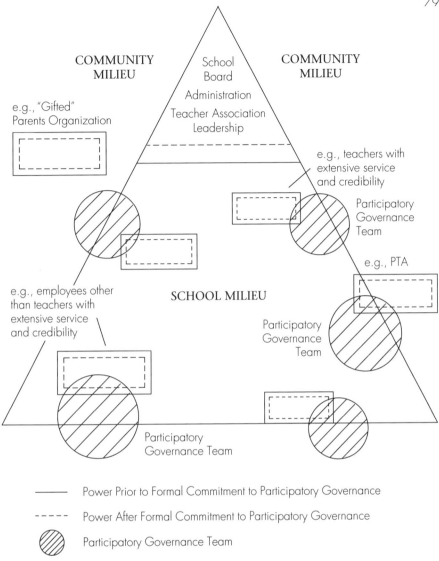

COMMUNITY
MILIEU

School
Board
Administration
Teacher Association
Leadership

COMMUNITY
MILIEU

e.g., "Gifted"
Parents Organization

e.g., teachers with
extensive service
and credibility

Participatory
Governance
Team

e.g., PTA

e.g., employees other
than teachers with
extensive service
and credibility

SCHOOL MILIEU

Participatory
Governance
Team

Participatory
Governance Team

———— Power Prior to Formal Commitment to Participatory Governance

- - - - - Power After Formal Commitment to Participatory Governance

Participatory Governance Team

Authority and Power Shift As a Result of Participatory Governance

This chart reflects the bureaucratic organizational structure of a public school system before and after formal commitment to a participatory governance. The participatory governance teams assume new authority and power, while existing organizations and those who derive their authority from the bureaucratic organizations will lose some power.

ture forth. They would do less harm to the organization to refuse formalized empowerment rather than commit in half measure.

The Creation of a Set of Involvement Processes

Once significant commitment of the major bureaucratic players has been secured, the next essential step to successful implementation is the creation of a set of involvement processes that will culminate in a community-generated definition of the purpose of schools. (See Chapter 2 for more specific information regarding the district's mission statement.)

One of the major shortcomings of school-based participatory governance teams in the late seventies and throughout the eighties was the absence of a community focus. The purpose (or "what") of public education must belong to the entire community, the large group from which the members of site-based teams ultimately will be selected. The site-based team is responsible for the "how" of improvement, and their school-level visions of excellence must complement the district purpose that they helped create.

Establishing the purpose of education is a task that will take at least a full year and possibly longer, especially if extensive involvement of the entire community is intended. Those involved should understand that this step cannot be done in haste. The process of measuring community attitudes is essential. A well-constructed survey of citizens, parents, teachers, students, and staff is a good place to begin. Respondents can be asked to prioritize the skills and values they feel children need to have as they complete their formal public school education. The process of measuring community attitudes is essential.

The next plan of community action should solicit the participation of many of the smaller diverse groups that will meet throughout the community. These meetings need to be held after the surveys have been collected and the results tabulated. At these meetings, the results can be shared and further discussions regarding the purpose of education can take place. Sometimes, the surveys and the meetings happen simultaneously throughout a community.

At some point, all the information from the surveys and the meetings needs to be brought to a large representative group that will fashion the language for the mission statement. The members of this group need to understand clearly that their task is not a creative one but rather the act of carefully synthesizing everything presented in the surveys and the meetings so that the mission statement represents the best and most coherent thinking of the entire community.

Although site-based teams can be formed and team members can be receiving training while the district purpose or mission is being formulated, it is far better, more focused, and less confusing to the district if the purpose or mission is established first.

STEP THREE

The Establishment of Parameters of Authority and Responsibility

If you advise any group of a hundred people that your school is moving toward shared decision making, you are likely to have a hundred different interpretations of what that means. Most people assume that shared decision making will result in more authority for those at the lower end of the bureaucracy and less authority for those at the top of the bureaucracy. Few would see this as having any adverse impact upon the existing authority or power they hold, unless they hold traditional positions such as principal, administrator, superintendent, or school board member.

In reality, however, virtually everyone in an organization holds some power, and the commitment to shared decision making might eventually affect everyone connected to the organization. Most people in an organization

Not Too Fast

Some years ago, as one district was beginning to make the commitment to shared decision making, the high school football coach said to the superintendent with obvious enthusiasm, "I'm really excited about this commitment to participatory governance."

"Why is that, coach?" the superintendent asked.

"Now we can finally be involved in the decisions that only the principal used to make," the coach replied.

"Coach," the superintendent countered, "I am so glad that you are enthusiastic about this commitment because last week your booster club came to me and said that next year they would like to be involved in selecting your first string players."

The coach looked puzzled and then, almost in a panic, exclaimed, "Well let's not go too fast with this thing."

— *RJG*

forget that they personally control some aspect of organizational decision making. Otherwise no organization could function.

It must be understood, however, that as the philosophy of participation begins to take hold, any former area of exclusive decision making may be challenged and most assuredly will be unless parameters are put in place up front in the process. Even with jurisdictional parameters in place, challenges may occur, although they will be less likely if the established parameters are perceived as reasonable. Ultimately, the participatory governance process itself and the site-based team will reallocate authority and responsibilities. The reallocation cannot (and should not) be forecast in advance since every community will make decisions based on their own particular needs.

Probably the most important role-setting parameters to establish in the beginning is a board policy that defines the conditions under which participatory governance has been endorsed. Such policies can be very specific or they can be more general. If policies are written with great specificity, the school system will experience less chaos as it moves toward shared decision making. However, the down side of great specificity is that the evolution toward more involvement will probably not occur unless those in traditional positions of power review their parameters at least annually, and consciously give up more bureaucratic power with each review. In districts where this annual review is not done, the evolution of involvement tends to stop. We, therefore, support less stringent parameters, even though this is more difficult because of the initial confusion that ensues.

Districts that may wish to set more stringent parameters should consider generating a minimum of three lists.

1. The first list should spell out very precisely what a site-based team can handle without needing to secure permission. For example, the authority to modify or change specific instructional strategies might be on this list.

2. The second list should spell out very precisely those areas a site-based team can examine but not implement change without permission from either the superintendent or the school board. For example, the authority to use textbooks other than those adopted by the state or local school board might be on this list. The existence of this list tends to protect the integrity of the decision making done by the traditional bureaucracy, while allowing for controlled and approved waiver deviations from such decisions. If this particular waiver mechanism is not in place, teams can deviate at will from school board policy, which could lead to organizational anarchy or, at a minimum, a school board that will experience increasing discomfort with its own creation. This list will also clearly delineate the decisions that are building-level authorizations as opposed to corporate authorizations, for as the first and second

list items are generated, gray areas of decision making will emerge that have never been properly assigned.

3. The third list should spell out very precisely which areas of decision making the site-based teams cannot be involved in. This list should delineate the laws or regulations to which schools and school systems must adhere. Included should be such federal laws as the amended P.L. 94-142 (legislation that guarantees all children, regardless of disability, a free and appropriate public education) and Supreme Court decisions such as *Goss v. Lopez*, which in 1975 elevated formal education to the level of property rights. Those areas of decision making that the district is not yet prepared to give up should also be included.

THESE THREE LISTS represent a more stringent approach to participatory governance, an approach that can be even more structured. For example, the list that applies to building level authority can be further subdivided into three lists: a list of building-level decisions that clearly belong to the governance team; a second list of building-level decisions that belong to the principal with consultation and input sought from the team; and a third list that represents building-level decisions that will be made by the principal alone.

We know of several districts in the country using such stringent and structured models. As we suggested earlier, this more zealous structure leaves less ambiguity, but at the cost of more spontaneous evolution. Whether or not lists are generated, districts need to develop a written policy regarding the position of the school board relative to site-based authority and the parameters under which such authority is given. The lack of written parameters leads to immense confusion regarding what is meant by participatory governance within the district and can lead to the creation of counterproductive conditions.

The policy should include five elements that we believe to be essential in defining what is meant by shared decision making:

SECTION ONE

The first policy element should express some philosophical position tied to significant research. Our personal preference is the effective schools research, which provides both a framework and a research justification for the participatory commitment. (See the Introduction for more information about the effective schools research.)

SECTION TWO

The second policy element should express the particular process involvement model that the district is endorsing. Is it the process model suggested in this book in Chapter 3, Building Blocks? Is it the traditional IDEA process model? Or is it a model developed by the district itself? Whichever model is being used, it should be specified, along with the areas of authority being given to the site-based team.

SECTION THREE

A third element should specify which process conditions need to be met by team members as they develop a vision for an improved school community. Further, it is strongly recommended that when teams present their vision for improvement to the school board, they address specifically what these conditions are. The school board trustees can then ask questions that will determine the extent to which the following process parameters have been honored:

Parameter One
The school community vision of excellence and the implementation strategies to carry it out should move toward fulfilling some aspect of the

district mission, especially if the community has had a significant hand in creating the district mission.

Parameter Two

The team must show how it has secured extensive community ownership for its own vision. For example, which involvement strategies were used? (Note: The board should never be confronted in later meetings by significant numbers of community members who are opposed to the vision presented. This would be testimony to the lack of extensive or necessary ownership at the community level.)

Parameter Three

The team must present a sound philosophical basis for its vision and implementation strategies. This basis would necessitate either (1) a preponderance of current research, (2) a thorough justification for going against such research, or (3) a rationale for vision and implementation of strategies for which there is currently no definitive research available.

Parameter Four

The team should present an assessment plan that shows the community and the school board how they plan to assess the effectiveness of their venture.

Parameter Five

The team should express how its new vision and implementation strategies will impact (if at all) schools who send them students (lower grade levels) or schools who receive their students (higher grade levels).

Parameter Six

No member of the site-based team should have veto power.

SECTION FOUR

The fourth policy element should deal with commitments at the district level. These should include:

- A commitment to allow for waivers from local board policies if necessary

- A commitment to provide any necessary information to site-based team members

- A commitment to offer participatory governance to new schools that may come into existence later

SECTION FIVE

A fifth and final element is recommended: A section that cautions districts to remember that the primary purpose of a participatory governance team is extended ownership and not the creation of new local bureaucracies.

SCHOOL BOARD MEMBERS should understand how the proposed site plan provides process guarantees. If the team can assure such guarantees, then the school board need not vote on approving the plan. In fact, voting at this time would unnecessarily diminish the authority and responsibility of the site-based teams. It would appear to relegate the authority of the teams to that of an advisory or a permission-seeking body. It would also unnecessarily burden the board with the responsibility of the newly created local vision. However, school board trustees must understand that they do give up authority over the plan itself. For some trustees, this is quite difficult.

Over the past ten years, we have developed and refined the sample board policy that follows. This sample policy, with modification, is being used successfully in school districts in Arizona, Idaho, Minnesota, Arkansas, Illinois, and Florida.

SAMPLE BOARD POLICY
Site-Based Shared Decision Making

SECTION ONE

Extensive research in education over the past twenty years has now culminated in a much clearer understanding of what makes an effective school. An effective school, as defined by this research, is a school where learning is occurring at high levels regardless of the cultural and economic background of the students. Further, this same research makes it clear that the largest unit of effective school improvement is not the school district, but rather the individual school community when the school community has at minimum the following characteristics:

- Consensus on explicit instructional goals, values, and beliefs (mission statement)

- District-level support for school improvement (board and administrative commitment to the effective schools research and the mission statement)

- Ongoing school-wide staff development training

- High level of parental involvement and support

- Individual school autonomy and flexibility

- Collaborative, collegial instructional planning

- Focus on basic skills acquisition

- Emphasis on higher order cognitive skills

- Teacher responsibility for instructional and classroom management decisions

- Teacher/parent accountability and acceptance of responsibility for student performance

- A safe, orderly, and disciplined school climate

- Strong instructional leadership

- Frequent monitoring of student progress

[Note: These are only some of the characteristics of effective schools.]

SECTION TWO

In response to this clear research, the school district now endorses and supports the Institute for the Development of Educational Activities (IDEA) process model of school improvement, a building-based shared decision-making model that creates the mechanism whereby a number of the characteristics of effective schools can become a reality. This incorporates notably high levels of parental involvement and support, individual school autonomy and flexibility, collaborative, collegial instructional planning and teacher/parent accountability and acceptance of responsibility for student performance. The board of education approves the implementation of this process model and further extends to site-based teams the authority to create curricular/instructional designs that meet the unique learning needs of the children served at each school.

New curricular/instructional designs have only the limitations that they be consistent and fulfill the mission statement.

Visions and implementation strategies must be arrived at through a process of consensus involving members of the school community.

continued on page 90

continued from page 89

The process being endorsed by this board must be understood to be an evolution of change, not a revolution. Authority extended to individual schools does not supersede traditional corporate decision making except in specific areas. As this process of change matures, the board is prepared to extend to site-based teams additional areas such as staffing, finances, and staff community development.

SECTION THREE

The board endorses this site-based process model contingent upon site-based teams fulfilling the following process elements:

1. School community visions of excellence and implementation strategies should move toward fulfilling some aspect of the district mission.

2. Each site-based team must demonstrate how they have involved their community in the creation of the vision and how extensive ownership within their community now exists for vision and implementation strategies.

3. Each site-based team needs to demonstrate how its vision and implementation strategies are supported.

4. Each site-based team must present an assessment plan identifying how they plan to evaluate the effectiveness of their venture.

5. Each site-based team must show evidence that it has made schools who are sending students to their site or will be receiving students from other sites aware of their particular vision and implementation designs even though their vision and

implementation design need not be modified or affected by such schools.

6. No member of the site-based team shall have veto power, nor will any building-level school administrator have veto power.

SECTION FOUR

If a particular site-based team's design plan conflicts with an existing board-approved program or policy, the board will first expect the site-based team to attempt to design an alternative plan that arrives at the same intended outcome without violation or conflict with the board-approved program or policy. If this cannot be accomplished, the board is prepared to consider waiver requests of existing board-approved programs or policies. If a plan requires waivers, it must be brought by the superintendent to the board of education for approval as a pilot program for the following school year. Waivers will be granted for one to four years and will be evaluated in light of the plan's ability to better serve the mission statement or purpose.

The process of building-based shared decision making works best when participants are provided with current research so that decisions made are based upon the best information available. There will be a conscious and ongoing effort on the part of the school corporation to provide site-based teams access to such current information. Further it is the responsibility of those actually involved in school improvement decision making to request and then to become familiar with this research information in order to ensure continuous improvement. This is not intended to limit a team's vision or implementation strategies to specific research.

continued on page 92

continued from page 91

The board of school trustees may, over time, endorse the creation of additional sites or schools. This may occur as a result of expanded enrollment or alternative schools or schools within a school. The board of education will extend its site-based shared decision making policies to any additional schools/sites that may come to exist.

SECTION FIVE

There is a tendency for site-based teams to lose their understanding of extended ownership and to become in effect a new local bureaucracy. Therefore, we must constantly be aware and remind one another that the movement to shared decision making at the school community level is not for the purpose of creating new, smaller bureaucracies to replace a larger bureaucracy but rather to involve all constituencies in our effort to fulfill the district mission statement or purpose.

IF A SCHOOL DISTRICT chooses this more general policy as opposed to the specific lists outlined earlier, then an additional parameter needs to be discussed and put in place. The necessity of this additional parameter may best be expressed by sharing the following story of an event that occurred some five years ago in a district where site-based teams had general policy-making authority over curriculum and instruction, without lists that specifically identified which curricular instructional areas belonged to the teams.

Several days before school began, the superintendent received a phone call from one of the building principals. The principal advised the superintendent that he was concerned because school was scheduled to start in three days and he had no books for the new school year. The superintendent asked whose primary responsibility it was to order the books. The principal replied, "I don't know. We are site-based and it is a curricular design."

The superintendent mobilized the district and made sure books were available for the first day of school. A condition of significant disruption was narrowly avoided.

To avoid such near misses, the following approach should be put into place on a district-wide level to ensure that such potential disruptions to an orderly organization do not occur: If the board approves the more general authority approach, say in the areas of curriculum and instruction, then site-based teams and others in the organization need to understand that the teams may focus on whichever area of curriculum and/or instruction their vision requires. *Once they choose an area — for example, mathematics, authentic assessment, portfolios, reading, or thematic units — then the responsibility for all other instructional areas will be carried out by those who carried out these responsibilities before.* In later years, site-based teams may take on additional authorities in curriculum and instruction. Again, however, whatever they do not take on will continue to be handled by those who previously handled the tasks.

STEP FOUR
Participatory Governance Training

The district is now ready to begin participatory governance training. Team selection and formation can take place before training, but if the district is prepared to make the commitment to train more than just the team members then team selection and formation can be postponed until after initial training has taken place. Ideally, training should be provided for virtually everyone employed by the district, as well as many parents, students, and community members. After the training, each school community should then be asked to form its team. (See Chapter 3 for more information about team building.)

Initial training sessions normally take two full days and seem to work best when the participants represent the broad-based constituencies of the community. Those who actually conduct the training should include people from the community who represent the community's diversity in as many ways as possible. A professional trainer may be employed as a consultant who mobilizes several teachers, parents, administrators, students, and board members to assist in aspects of this training. This models from the beginning of the training the more extensive ownership sought in the participatory process.

At some point early in the training — perhaps on the first day — the participants should hear school board trustees, the superintendent, and presidents or executive officers of employee associations express their genuine commitment to the process being initiated.

The training should cover the following topics:

1. An explanation of the effective schools research, particularly those elements that can be enhanced by the establishment of participatory governance at the individual school level.

2. A thorough explanation of the meaning and intent of the district mission or purpose. This is best accomplished by asking those participants in the training sessions who actually had a significant role in the formation of the district mission statement to present this section of the training. Ideally, all had some hand in such formation, so finding participants who were involved should not be difficult.

3. A thorough review of the process elements endorsed and supported by the district for the functioning of the site-based teams. If pyramiding, visioning, and consensus building are endorsed and supported, then participants need to have a thorough understanding of these processes.

4. A detailed coverage of the general authority and responsibility initially being given to teams, with an explanation of waiver mechanisms and the specific conditions if the district has elected to structure more tightly.

5. A thorough discussion of the parameters that teams must follow in order to move forward with a school plan.

6. Resources where team members can access databases and acquire needed information in order to study issues they may wish to consider. An impressive information source has been developed in recent years under the direction of Dr. Maggie Mangini of Arizona State University's College of Education.[1] Called the Arizona Education Information System, the group researches and keeps current more than five hundred educational topics such as nongraded schools, portfolio assessment, and cooperative learning. Districts can purchase their services for various levels of access and thus quickly provide teams with researched information on almost any topic.

   Teams should take advantage of local resources as well. School districts have personnel who can provide information or direct team members to places where they can access information. Many communities also have extensions of state universities, which can be a valuable source of information. Further, many libraries have in place an information system that can provide information and generate lists of resources.

7. The importance of an annual review of the transition to participatory governance, including an evaluation of progress and a determination of whether or not team members would like to continue to participate in the shared decision-making process.

8. An evaluation of the district's (or individual school's) capacity to fund on-going professional development.

Besides the initial training of all involved, a schedule of on-going trainings should be established for any new team members who become involved — for example, parents new to the community, staff new to the district, and community members newly interested in the process of participatory governance.

The Establishment of a System-Wide Communication Council

After the site-based teams are formed and functioning, a system-wide council should be established to facilitate communication between the schools in the district. This council should include at least one site-based team member from each school in the district and also some central office administrators, teacher association representatives, and possibly a representative from the district's parent-teacher association.

While most school systems run quite efficiently and uniformly, after participatory governance this may not be the case. In particular, district personnel will experience an increased demand for information. For example, prior to the implementation of site-based governance, the curriculum guide for the third grade is created at the district level and used with only slight modifications at schools within a district. As site-based plans of action are implemented, the "how" of public education from one school to another within the district probably will begin to take on unique forms and twists. Teachers, administrators, and parents who formerly were satisfied with knowing only what was going on in their own school will begin to want increased information about what is going on in other schools since a wider range of educational practices is now in use at different sites. This new demand for information becomes particularly acute during the second and third years of district-level involvement in site-based governance. During these years in particular, some schools will have already formulated and implemented their plan while others are still seeking their way.

The system-wide communication council provides a meaningful and necessary monthly exchange of information and works well as long as the representatives on the council understand that their clear charge is to take back to their schools all they have heard. By the fourth year of implementation, this demand for information begins to subside, in part because the district is becoming more comfortable with diversity and in part because each school community is developing a comfort level with its own choices. Even in later years, though perhaps meeting less frequently, the communication council should be maintained as it provides a forum for meaningful communication.

Note

1. Arizona Education Information System (AEIS) Gold Files, Arizona State University, College of Education, Bureau of Education Research and Services, (800) 624-2347.

FIVE

Stumbling Blocks

WHEN A DISTRICT BEGINS to implement site-based participatory governance, some people become very excited about the possibilities that seem open to them. "Finally," they think, "we'll be able to make changes. We'll get in there and get the job done and get it done quickly. We can get rid of the old-fashioned ways. Now that principal [or the superintendent or the school board] will have to listen to us."

Others will be more leery. They will be suspicious of this shift of power. Will empowerment really occur or will this be just another situation where input is sought but no real authority to make decisions is provided? Will some members of the site-based team have more power than others? If someone does not like the direction a site-based team is taking, can that team be stopped?

A few people will anticipate overwhelming confusion. Unclear about authority and responsibility, they suspect that the district will become an administrative nightmare. They are uneasy about the empowerment of people who might lack the necessary expertise. They admit that things are not perfect and that improvement is needed, but they are not at all sure this is the way to bring about such change or improvement.

Evolution of the kind we are proposing invariably means the simultaneous existence of two organizations: the traditional bureaucracy giving up authority and responsibility in a controlled manner and a new emerging organization comprised of empowered multiple constituent groups. This gradual phasing out of the old while phasing in the new brings with it some predictable complexities. The following stumbling blocks are the direct result of the commitment to participatory governance. Besides identifying these potentially troublesome areas, we suggest numerous strategies that we believe will alleviate the most common difficulties. These stumbling blocks are presented as questions that frequently are asked by those considering the shift toward shared decision making, accompanied by answers based on the experiences of those who have successfully navigated through the transition phase to participatory governance.

If I join a site-based team, what authority and responsibilities will I have?

The reallocation of authority and responsibilities will vary from district to district, depending on state law and district policy, as well as union contracts. Each system can look to its own state department of education, as well as teacher organizations and state school board associations or administrative organizations for possible suggestions on responsibilities. These same sources will also be helpful in providing ideas regarding visioning, especially in indicating which other school districts are engaging in participatory governance and which school sites might welcome visitors who seek information about site-based management. But remember, visions will be unique to each community. The members of site-based teams will probably be more interested in information about curriculum, school culture, student assistance programs like conflict resolution, mainstreaming, and professional staff development.

Once we get started with participatory governance, how long will it take to see improvements?

Many people assume that when a school shifts toward participatory governance, the results should be quickly evident or should occur within a predictable time frame, especially in areas where problems have been obvious. For this reason, people will naturally ask how long it will take to see the improvements. When people ask this question, they are assuming that the improvement of a school means simply that something is broken and can be fixed once and for all. But can we really compare the current state of any given public school with a broken toaster or a bent bicycle frame?

We often make the same erroneous assumption when we talk about health. Unless a person has a disease or is somehow impaired, we assume that nothing is wrong and that the person is healthy. However, an insightful observation is offered by Scott Peck in *A World Waiting to Be Born* when he compares the health of a human body to the health of an organization. This will help us understand the fallacious attitude revealed by the question "How long will it take?"

> *The point that health is not so much the* absence *of disease as it is the* presence *of an optimal healing process is crucial for understanding our lives. It is crucial because the principle applies not only to our physical health but also to our mental health and to the health of our organizations and institutions. A healthy organization — whether a marriage, a family, or a business operation — is not one with an absence of problems, but one that is actively and effectively addressing or healing its problems.*[1]

We share this passage because it confronts the mind-set that so many of us have about schools. We tend to see them as physical entities that we can examine, diagnose, correct, and be done with. This is not the case. Schools are living things just as society is a living thing, both being highly dynamic and evolutionary. There will never be an end point. We will never be "done with it."

What about funding? Are there front-end expenses that should be considered?

Several years ago I was asked to speak to a legislative body in one of our western states. At the time the legislators were contemplating whether or not to mandate that every school in their state move toward site-based governance. I began my presentation by complimenting the general assembly on their willingness to spend additional millions for public education. I also cautioned them that successful implementation cannot take place unless those charged with creating visions and new ways of approach are given much more than we have ever given them in terms of professional development opportunities. After my presentation, the legislation was modified. The legislators were not willing to endorse such spending.

A major stumbling block that will become apparent as schools move toward participatory governance is the dramatic difference that exists between the public school sector and the successful business industrial sector with respect to the amount of resources made available for professional development activities. According to most estimates, the average school system in the United States is currently spending less than 1 percent of its budget on professional development. Successful organizations in the business industrial sector currently spend between 7 and 9 percent of their budget in this same area. They understand that improvement cannot occur in a meaningful way unless significant resources are used for the growth and development of those people in their organization who are on the front line.

I used to be the principal. What do I do now?

There is probably no more difficult role to perform in a school district than that of building principal. Responsibility for the total operation of that building falls on the principal's shoulders, yet rarely does the principal have the resources necessary to adequately perform that function. If the district has any discretionary resource authority, it is in the hands of the central office, the superintendent and/or the school board. Most building principals, clearly understanding this, walk back into their building daily and continue to try their best to provide a quality education.

If any role is perceived as particularly vulnerable following the onset of school-based management, it is the role of the building principal. Most schools that involve the sharing of decision making at the building level have the appearance of adversely impacting the principal's already misunderstood authority and role. Therefore, prior to any movement toward the initiation of school-based management, considerable time should be spent discussing with building principals the implications of a new design on their role and authority.

In addition, the trustees and the superintendent need to modify their authority consistent with their expectations for authority and role modification at the building level. If, for example, the superintendent holds the exclusive authority to interview and recommend for hiring all employees, then the superintendent should consider sharing such authority with any school-based operation. Modifications made by the board and the central office authorities can send a clear message of commitment, particularly to those front line administrators who are so important to the successful implementation of participatory governance.

One of the tragedies inherent in the collective perception about education is that schools are thought of as assembly lines where each individual has a function to perform and the result is a product that fully meets all pre-designed expectations. Parents, teachers, and building administrators all unconsciously tend to use that same industrial-based, assembly line model when they think of the operations of schools. When faced with the possibility of collaborative decision making, a principal usually sees the potential for a forced distortion of what was his or her role. Yet all the building principals I have ever encountered could easily generate an extensive listing of the things they would like to do — in fact, would prefer to do — if time permitted. The move to participatory governance should allow principals to have more time and the opportunity to focus on those things they've been wanting to do. This would most certainly enhance their role as educational leaders in the true sense.

Is it possible for a school community to follow a district's parameters and come up with a plan that a board member or a superintendent doesn't like?

To endorse school-based decision making is to endorse a process that involves divergent constituent groups in the creation of what they collectively believe is better. The end result of their work will not be known by them or the traditional authorities of the school district until they are well into the process. It is inevitable that some school community will create a vision or endorse an implementation strategy that was unpredictable, sometimes grating upon the normal decision makers of the district.

At that point, the entire district will focus on what happens next. The issue will become a district-wide issue, even though the school-based team has religiously followed the process. Traditional authority's commitment to participatory governance will be at stake. If veto power is introduced, the new design will effectively be killed because veto power moves the school-based team back to the advisory committee status, which requires only a stapled, written report to those who have the real authority and allows for no action. Any board or superintendent who moves toward participatory governance must be prepared to accept a newly created vision that may not be to their liking.

I've been on committees before. How is this one going to be any different?

I have not been anywhere in the country where school-based teams have not begun to slip back into more familiar and therefore more comfortable committee structure designs. Some members of school-based teams may have taken part in an initial training where they were introduced to the techniques outlined in Chapter 3:

- Human development activities to build higher levels of trust

- Pyramiding procedures to gain extended ownership of eventual designs

- Techniques to ensure that the school-based team is made up of persons who represent divergent groups and divergent thinking

Unfortunately, training in these techniques is usually available to only a handful of the people who ultimately will make up a larger, more extensive school-based group. The trained members of the school-based team are often a minority of the total group that eventually makes up that team. It is often erroneously assumed that those who have been trained will carry the participatory process in its pure form back to the larger group. Whether or not this occurs depends upon the ability of those trained to carry out this function. Often the power of mind-sets regarding how committees function is stronger than the initial training in the new processes. For this reason, it is not at all uncommon to find, even six months after initial training, that school-based teams have modified or totally eliminated the process elements that are really critical to successful participatory governance.

Members of site-based teams who have personal knowledge of institutional committee structure and functioning will have an especially difficult time. This, coupled with the probability that the majority of team members have not been directly involved in training, leads to the inevitable. The team begins to function like a traditional committee.

The pyramid process element is usually the first to go. For various reasons, building by building, other elements begin to fade away within the first year. The larger the school district, the more likely this is to occur, particularly if the school district begins site-based management with a large number of schools. There seems to be a common lack of acceptance, nationwide, of the fact that some kind of significant monitoring and/or support system is critical to the successful functioning of a new participatory governance team.

Vigilance is needed to prevent this erosion of the commitment to shared decision making. A site-based team is not the same as the traditional committee. The members of the site-based team are charged with forming designs of improvement that are responsive to the total community. The site-based team does not act in an advisory capacity, nor does it take action in isolation. The members of the team do not arrive at decisions by voting. The processes in which team members are trained must be maintained to ensure that the purpose for the team's formation is fulfilled.

We must rely on more than the hope that those who are trained can motivate the entire group to function with a thorough understanding of how participatory governance works. This may mean setting up procedures for monitoring progress and providing opportunities for periodically revisiting the training. Watching for the stumbling blocks described here and taking these preventive steps may make the road less rocky:

1. Make sure that everyone understands how authorities and responsibilities are delineated.

2. Allow for sufficient time for training so that questions regarding all the implications of participatory governance may be addressed.

3. Establish open lines of communication so that people in any part of the organization who need further explanation or clarification can be assisted in a timely and comprehensive fashion.

4. Have a mechanism in place so that questions, whether logistical or philosophical, that arise after training can be discussed. Designate one or more individuals within the organization to assume this responsibility. Choose someone who is familiar with the workings of the organization as well as with participatory governance processes. This person can also be asked to keep the group focused and on task.

5. Establish a group to meet on a routine and frequent basis specifically to address any concerns about participatory government or the changes that have resulted from site-based management.

A final suggestion is that each district needs to have in place ways to lessen confusion and mechanisms to keep communication flowing. First, a district needs to take as many preventive steps as possible, making sure that everyone understands how authorities and responsibilities are delineated.

Note

1. M. Scott Peck, *A World Waiting to Be Born: Civility Rediscovered* (New York: Bantam, 1993), p. 10.

SIX

Some Blocks Left Over

Site-Based Budgeting and Staffing

Participatory governance at the site level is often restricted to such areas as curriculum, instructional techniques, and school culture, but if participatory governance is truly evolutionary, shared decision making should evolve into such areas as budgeting and staffing. On the surface, this evolution may seem impossible. How can budgeting and staffing be accomplished in an orderly and responsible manner, maintaining district-level responsibility to the community while at the same time providing significant authority and equitable treatment to school sites? To answer this question, a set of almost uniform national educational conditions needs to be reviewed.

First, in virtually every school district in the country, 85 to 91 percent of the district's general fund is used to pay salaries and benefits of employees. Thus, to truly control a school's budget is to control staffing. A number of school districts involved in site-based budgeting have in actuality given the site-based teams authority over only a modicum of the budget — that small portion that controls materials and supplies, and perhaps another portion that controls staff development.

Second, in virtually every community but particularly in communities where one school board oversees a K–12 district, an inequitable distribution of money is apparent. High schools get the greatest amount per pupil, junior high or middle schools get somewhat less per pupil than high schools, and elementary schools receive the least per pupil. A naive reader might think, "Well, of course this is true. High school students need more financial support, if only for their extra-curricular activities." We would not attempt to justify such naive thinking to an astute group of elementary school teachers, for they would counter with arguments that include the obvious need for full-day kindergarten, the critical need for elementary level counselors and psychologists, the almost tearful plea for organized after-school activities, not to mention the need for supplementary art and music programs, physical education teachers and equipment, and additional classroom aides who can provide some essential one-on-one work with students who enter school two to three years behind in readiness skills.

If a district is seriously contemplating the evolutionary move to site-based budgeting and staffing, then a preliminary meeting with parents, teachers, and students is recommended. One of the first questions posed by members of that audience will justifiably be "Will there be an equitable distribution of district money to each school?" We suspect that if the answer is anything less than "Equal dollars for each pupil within the district regardless of grade level," the answer will not be well received. The movement to such equity will take time, for the money being spent now represents earlier decision-making priorities. With appropriate representation, the district will have to reassess its priorities.

If radical surgery is to be avoided, equity may take a number of years. In addition, once a reasonable level of equity is achieved, some unavoidable conditions — even between one elementary school and another — will skew the budget. For example, the level of professional experience at one school may be higher than at another, which will necessitate an adjustment in dollar allocation for salaries. Naturally, the number of students will have to be factored into the budget, but as a student/teacher ratio. One elementary school may have twenty-five fourth graders, requiring one teacher, while a neighboring school may have thirty-eight fourth graders, requiring two teachers. The salary allocation *per pupil* will not be equal.

The following suggestions will help those who are considering the issue of equity:

1. If site-based teams are to have authority over curriculum, they will ultimately need to have authority over staffing because the two areas are inextricably linked.

2. Any district that intends to move to site-based budgeting and staffing should assess the current monetary distribution and then, slowly and conscientiously, through new priorities, move in the direction of equitable distribution.

3. The definition of equitable distribution should be the basis for a number of dialogues among representatives of all affected parties, including school board trustees, central office administrators, association leadership, parents, students, and community members. Out of these sessions should come a definition of equitable distribution for the present and for the future, with a list of exceptions that are acceptable to all.

Any district that wishes to move quickly toward equity might consider implementing a policy that includes the site-based team in case-by-case decision making regarding placement. We suggest that when a vacancy exists in any school (whether the result of a resignation, retirement, or increased student enrollment), then the district personnel office will notify the site-based team, which has a choice of three options:

- Advise the personnel department to follow its existing policy and fill the position.

- Advise the personnel department that the site-based team will work with the personnel department to fill the position. The team will have access to applicants' files and will strive to fill the position as defined by the personnel department.

- Advise the personnel office that the site-based team, *with the support of the community,* intends to use the money available for that defined vacancy in some other way.

The third option is that of true participatory governance. Let's look at an example: The site-based team is advised that due to increased enrollment a position is open for a third grade teacher, but team members would rather use the funds to hire a counselor. If the team chooses to use the money in this new way, the team members — not the trustees or the administrators — bear the responsibility of explaining to the school community why third grade class sizes will be larger. In addition, team members and the school community need to understand that support for the new counselor came about because of increased revenue based on increased enrollment. Finally, if enrollment decreases to a level where a teaching position would normally be eliminated, then the team must decide which position to eliminate.

The Modern Student in Ancient Hallways

I vividly remember a time, years ago, when I was a new instructor hired to teach seventh grade math. I was given a seventh grade math book and told that the content of the text contained what my students needed to learn that year. My students began the school year with varying degrees of math skills — some students were struggling while a handful of others were already competent in all topics covered by the textbook.

I looked for supplementary books at the local library, in my own personal library, and at friends' houses. I brought into class a broad range of math-related materials and I asked my students to choose items that piqued their interest. The next few months were some of the most exciting and most chaotic months of teaching that I have ever

---

experienced. I could feel the learning occurring all around me, even though I periodically felt guilty because I wasn't teaching in any traditional sense. I was acting more like a facilitator or a resource person.

Halfway through the school year, I was called to the office of the principal, who was quite distressed. She advised me that I had violated one of the fundamental rules of curricular articulation. Some of my students were experimenting with mathematical concepts found appropriately only in the study of algebra and geometry. She further advised me that it was the school's practice, approved by the high school, to introduce these topics only to the brightest of the eighth grade students and only in the last quarter of their eighth grade year. She clearly told me to cease what I was doing and finally commented that she was reasonably confident that I would not be asked back the next year.

At that early stage of my career, I did not fully understand what I had done wrong. I know now that I had transgressed from what I call the architectural design of public education. For several years I was genuinely angry at this principal. Later, as I matured and learned more about the system, the anger drained away as I began to understand that it was actually the architecture that was to blame, an ancient architecture put in place by people addressing the educational needs of a previous generation of learners. Now it's obvious that we need to ask a pertinent question: Is that educational architecture still appropriate for today's learners, whose feet walk briskly through these ancient hallways?

— RJG

Ancient Architecture

Throughout our country and even beyond, the ancient educational architecture is securely in place. Constructed a little at a time over a long period of time, both thoughtfully and accidentally, this architecture bears such names as content-articulated curriculum, grade levels, textbooks and workbooks, semesters, report cards, independent learning, suspensions, expulsions, alternative schools, four-year high schools, and competitive sports. Because this architecture has been in place so very long, it now has the ownership of all those who, for better or worse, were required to experience it. Clearly, then, a change in the architecture of public education cannot take place without the knowing consent of all those who currently feel they own it.

Most businesses do not suffer this constraint to change. Their architecture is called production and, according to quality management theory, companies control their own production without reference to customers or constituencies. If management and employees find a need to modify production in order to make improvements, they do so. For example, if a company feels that changing to a four-day work week will improve productivity, management has no qualms about making such a change. Within the current architecture of schools, though, to make such a change — even if improvement were quite predictable — would require the support not only of administrators, teachers, school board trustees, parents, and all other members of the community who would be affected by such a change, but also of all those unaffected but plainly comfortable with the old architecture.

The control of public school architecture goes far beyond the principal who demanded an articulated, structured, and sequential curriculum for seventh grade math students. The control of American public education belongs to us all. As site-based team members gather within their communities to study school improvement, they need to try not to blame school board trustees, teachers, parents, or principals for the problems and shortcomings within their schools. Instead, they need to understand that although we have learned to accept a certain way of doing things, this ancient design may need to be revised to meet the changing needs of our children. Mostly, those committed to the reform of public education need to understand that when change is determined to be necessary, it will occur in a sustained fashion only if it comes with collective and informed consent.

Vision and Assessment

In his marvelous video *The Power of Vision,* Joel Barker says any company whose primary purpose (mission) is to make money probably never will, but a company whose primary purpose is customer satisfaction — once achieved — will make money.[1] From an educational perspective, we suggest the following principle holds. Any school district whose mission is to foster profound learning by simply focusing on raising standardized test scores never will, even though test scores may go up. For in order to foster such profound learning, a school district must address the total culture of the educational environment. When such school districts get children to believe in themselves, create school environments that result in the joy of learning, empower and encourage educators to take risks with new ideas, then profound learning will result and, *not incidentally,* test scores will go up. Experience in this area further suggests that the more a vision or purpose can be quantifiably measured by standardized tests, the less that vision or purpose is capable of resulting in or creating the more profound kind of learning children need to experience.

As an example, let's look at two radically different approaches to the improvement of reading skills:

1. The goal of improved reading skills is stated in terms of children learning specific reading strategies and a specific number of vocabulary words. The lessons focus on measurable outcomes related to decoding skills and the sight memorization of words.

2. The goal of improved reading skills is stated in terms of experiencing reading as fun, helpful, and empowering. The lessons focus on reading enjoyment, sound experimentation, story sharing, teaching others, choosing books to read, writing stories, and increasing word awareness and word meanings.

Either of these two approaches will raise test scores in reading, but are both approaches appropriate visions of education? We pose this question because we frequently find across the country school district after school district, and many times entire states, reluctant to create affective domain visions as represented by the second approach outlined above. This hesitation seems to occur because assessment cannot be easily accomplished when using the approach described in the second example. Unfortunately, since the traditional standardized tests cannot measure progress in these affective areas, too many schools fall back on the familiar assessment tools rather than create visions that call for new assessment techniques.

The new assessment techniques now in vogue look for what students can generate, demonstrate, and exhibit rather than what they can repeat. However, college requirements remain a major concern of many parents. Assessment changes cannot be made without full awareness of how colleges will respond. Participatory teams need to — in fact, are forced to — go very cautiously here.

Artists and the Art of Teaching

Several months ago, after dinner at home with our youngest son Tommy, we decided to watch some television in our den. We turned to the education channel emanating out of Muncie, Indiana, for Tommy is at that young age where he finds programs about fish or wildlife or volcanoes quite absorbing, and this particular channel has a lot of these programs. To our pleasant surprise, the station was airing a program we had not anticipated, entitled *Backstage/Lincoln Center.*[2] It revealed a marvelous keyhole view of the artists' attitudes toward their art and one another, both prior to and during performances. As the program unfolded, the focal point eventually came to rest upon Zubin Mehta, the conductor of the New York Philharmonic Orchestra. Moved to a state of awe by his sensitive and inspiring definition regarding what it means to be a leader, we were impressed with his clear understanding of the artists in front of him and what they need from a leader in order to most successfully perform their art, both individually and as a group.

Being educators, we immediately translated his message to schools — places we know to be filled with teachers, who are themselves artists, and we thought of principals, those former artists who are asked to conduct. We listened, almost spellbound, as Zubin Mehta expressed that his relationship with this body of artists is so much more than cognitive. He told how he watches them as they watch him until — at some point in the performance — they tell him, with a look or a glance, or through their eyes, to let go. He knows to do so, and at that point the music becomes their own and he, as conductor, simply holds them together.

The tape of this program was graciously given to us by the station and has been seen by all the administrators in our district. Extensive dialogue has followed as to its meaning for these former teacher/artists. They have come to understand that leaders must learn when to let go, and what it means to let go while they simply "hold them together." This understanding is critical if we intend to have our teachers' performances be those memorable ones that students will profit from and occasionally cherish.

I [RJG] remember and often cherish one such educational experience on a pleasant fall day that changed my life and view of the world forever. I was a sophomore in high school when one class discussion, emanating from an analysis of "Thanatopsis" by William Cullen Bryant, moved to an open dialogue regarding mortality — not a topic typically discussed by fifteen year olds — and I clearly remember the feeling that we had finally exhausted the topic and cognitively understood the concept of mortality.

Our teacher, Mr. Nelson, who often encouraged such classroom discussions, wasn't finished with the lesson. "I have one final question for you," he said.

Feeling quite comfortable that we could handle whatever he had in mind, we urged him on in an almost game-show manner: "Please, go ahead, ask us."

With virtually no emotion, he then said, "What would you do if your mother died?"

Momentarily puzzled, we looked at one another and then slowly yet still somewhat confidently we began to volunteer our answers:

"Call my relatives."

"Begin to make arrangements for the funeral."

"Check with the insurance company."

"Try to figure out if anyone had made previous cemetery arrangements."

Finally, Mr. Nelson turned to a student named Tony, who always sat in the far back corner of the classroom, next to the blackboard, and never volunteered. Most of the time he looked down at his desk and with his pencil just kind of drew a lot, but when we were engaged in class discussions, he clearly listened and even smiled now and then. We didn't dislike Tony. We never made fun of him or picked on him, but we knew he was a little slow.

Mr. Nelson walked slowly toward Tony and as he neared his desk, he asked again: "Tony, what would you do?"

Tony slowly looked up from his drawing and quietly said, "I'd cry."

Mr. Nelson touched Tony on the head, looked at us all, and said, "That's right, Tony. You'd cry."

A long silence came over the class. Mr. Nelson dismissed us early, which he sometimes did when he wanted us to reflect on the day's lesson, saying simply, "Bryant meant for you to feel, not merely understand."

That afternoon and many afternoons after that, several of us walked Tony home. He seemed to like that and we had learned something new to appreciate and respect in all the Tonys we would ever know. Mr. Nelson's performance was a memorable one, and we did profit and we did cherish the memory.

Years later I had the privilege of becoming a young administrator in that same district, and on one occasion had the pleasure of talking with a former principal who had come to a special tea to honor some retiring teachers with whom he had worked. We exchanged some pleasantries and then quite casually moved to a brief discussion regarding the evolving role of school administrators. As the brief discussion came to a close, he looked at me and said, "I hope one thing never changes — our understanding as administrators that the excellence of schools will continue only if those of us selected to administer schools never forget that at the heart of educational excellence is the daily creative interaction that exists between classroom teacher and pupils. I hope our role will forever be to assist in creating and nurturing school environments where that creative genius is enhanced, not stifled or crushed with what might appear to be the necessary requirements of bureaucracy."

If there is a final something worth passing on regarding new designs for schools, we believe it to be found in our understanding of artists, gained over the years: that creativity is the first child of freedom. As those who lead, we must remember to watch the eyes of our artists/teachers and know when to let go. If we don't learn to let go, all of the profound teachings that might have led to educational gains for children will not occur because such teaching will not be risked. This message we respectfully pass on to all newly formed site-based teams and all others who hold the awesome responsibility for our schools.

Notes

1. Joel Arthur Barker, *The Power of Vision* (Chart House International Learning Corporation, 221 River Ridge Circle, Burnsville, MN 55337; 1990, 30 minutes).

2. Leonard Slatkin, *Backstage/Lincoln Center* (A Production of Lincoln Center for the Performing Arts, Inc., 1994).

Suggested Readings

Barker, Joel Arthur. *Paradigms: The Business of Discovering the Future.* New York: HarperBusiness, 1993.

Brookover, Wilbur et al. *Creating Effective Schools: An In-Service Program for Enhancing School Learning Climate and Achievement.* Holmes Beach, FL: Learning Publications, 1982.

Collins, Marva, and Civia Tamarkin. *Marva Collins' Way: Returning to Excellence in Education.* Los Angeles: J. P. Tarcher, 1990.

Csikszentmihalyi, Mihaly. *Flow: The Psychology of Optimal Experience.* New York: HarperCollins, 1991.

Deming, W. Edwards. *Out of the Crisis.* Cambridge, MA: MIT Center for Advanced Engineering Study, 1986.

Deming, W. Edwards. *The New Economics for Industry, Government, Education.* Cambridge, MA: MIT Center for Advanced Engineering Study, 1992.

Gardner, Howard. *Frames of Mind: The Theory of Multiple Intelligence.* New York: Basic Books, 1985.

Gatto, John Taylor. *Dumbing Us Down: The Hidden Curriculum of Compulsory Schooling.* Philadelphia: New Society, 1992.

Gould, Stephen Jay. *The Mismeasure of Man.* New York: W. W. Norton, 1983.

Grosse, Carol, and Terri Fields. *The Best Kept Secret to Achieving Successful School Management* (Phoenix: Innovative Materials, 1986). To order by mail, send $10 plus $1.50 for postage and handling to Innovative Materials, 3142 E. Rose Lane, Phoenix, AZ 85016.

Guterson, David. *Family Matters: Why Homeschooling Makes Sense.* New York: Harcourt Brace Jovanovich, 1992.

Hart, Leslie A. *Human Brain and Human Learning.* Village of Oak Creek, AZ: Books for Educators, 1983.

Kozol, Jonathan. *Savage Inequities: Children in America's Schools.* New York: HarperCollins, 1992.

Lezotte, Lawrence W. *Creating the Total Quality Effective School.* Okemos, MI: Effective School Products, Ltd., 1992.

Lezotte, Lawrence W., and Barbara C. Jacoby. *A Guide to the School Improvement Process Based on Effective Schools Research.* Okemos, MI: Effective School Products, Ltd., 1990.

Lezotte, Lawrence W., and Barbara C. Jacoby. *Sustainable School Reform: The District Context for School Improvement.* Okemos, MI: Effective School Products, Ltd., 1992.

Marzano, Robert J. *A Different Kind of Classroom: Teaching with Dimensions of Learning.* Alexandria: Association for Supervision and Curriculum Development, 1992.

Mathews, Jay. *Escalante: The Best Teacher in America.* New York: Henry Holt and Company, 1989.

Pauly, Edward. *Classroom Crucible: What Really Works, What Doesn't, and Why.* New York: Basic Books, 1992.

Peck, M. Scott. *A World Waiting to Be Born: Civility Rediscovered.* New York: Bantam, 1993.

Phillips, Gary, and Maurice Gibbons. *63 Ways of Improving Classroom Instruction.* Issaquah, WA: National School Improvement Project, ca. 1984.

Senge, Peter M. *Fifth Discipline: Mastering the Five Practices of the Learning Organization*. New York: Doubleday, 1990.

Toch, Thomas. *In the Name of Excellence: The Struggle to Reform the Nation's Schools and Why It's Failing and What Should Be Done*. New York: Oxford University Press, 1991.

United States Department of Labor, Secretary's Commission on Achieving Necessary Skills (SCANS). "What Work Requires of Schools: A SCANS Report for America 2000." Washington, D.C.: United States Department of Labor, 1991.

Index

About the Authors

MARION J. GOLARZ has both a bachelor's degree and a master's degree in education from Indiana University. Her professional experiences are varied and include the teaching of English and special education at the high school level, composition at the university level, and remedial reading with Chapter 1 students at the elementary and middle school levels.

RAYMOND J. GOLARZ holds both a bachelor's degree in sociology and a bachelor's degree in education from St. Joseph's College in Indiana. He received a master's degree and a doctorate in education from Indiana University. He has taught at the elementary, middle school, high school, and university levels.

Dr. Golarz has been an administrator in three Indiana school systems. In 1984 he was appointed assistant superintendent in Hammond. From 1986 to 1989 he was the superintendent in Hobart. In 1989 he accepted a position as superintendent of the Richmond Community Schools in Richmond. In all three school systems he helped introduce and develop participatory governance.

Due to his vast experience in school improvement coupled with his unique speaking ability, there is an extensive demand for Dr. Golarz's keynote speeches and workshop presentations. He has worked with school and community personnel representing more than three thousand school districts throughout the United States and Canada, and he is an international presenter on participatory governance for Phi Delta Kappa.

RAY AND MARION trace their interest in education to their own school experiences and to the unique value placed on education by their grandparents, who immigrated to the United States, seeking a better life for their children and grandchildren. Because of their long professional involvement and belief that education can change lives for the better, they are familiar with the successes and the difficulties that are part of the current struggle on the part of public school educators to improve education for all children. It is their own children and the children of their extended families, friends, and neighbors, however, who have made them most profoundly aware of the potential of schools to be very positive for some, while harmful for others.

Over the years it has become increasingly clear to these educators that in every community people from all backgrounds remain hopeful that their children will learn and succeed in school. It has also become clear that far too many people — both educators and parents — feel awkward, intimidated, or helpless when attempting to voice their concerns or raise educational issues within the framework of the traditional educational bureaucracy. They hope that by becoming involved in participatory governance, all citizens will be helping local schools become a place where all children feel safe, acquire the necessary tools to sustain a lifelong search for knowledge, and feel free to explore their destiny.

RAY AND MARION may be contacted at P.O. Box 7197, Bloomington, Indiana 47407, phone (812) 333-1997.

About National Training Associates

NATIONAL TRAINING ASSOCIATES (NTA) is a training and consultation firm comprised of educational specialists who are dedicated to encouraging the personal, organizational, and social change that fosters generational wellness for children, families, and communities. Since 1982 NTA has provided training and consultation services to assist school communities in planning, organizing, implementing, and evaluating comprehensive student assistance programs. From a genesis in drug/alcohol identification and intervention to the current emphasis on community-based planning and school restructuring, NTA is continually evolving its services to meet the changing needs of schools and the communities they serve.

The services offered by NTA are best viewed from the perspective of how they address the specific needs identified by a school, business, or community. Central to NTA's overall approach is the development and nourishment of teams and community partnerships, with the focus on enhancing the lives of youth of all ages. Training, technical assistance, and consultation are offered in three of the four areas outlined below. In the fourth area, NTA acts as an events-facilitator.

Safe Schools and Communities
Community Mobilization
Safety and Violence Prevention
Managing Aggression
Youth Empowering Systems (YES)
Peer Mediation

Building Influence with Youth

Building Student Resiliency

Nonverbal Classroom Management Techniques

Parents As Advocates

Mentor Training

Building Rapport with High-Risk Youth

Educational Coach Training

Building Self-Sufficiency

Site-Based Management and School Restructuring

Building Individual Leadership Potential

Facilitating High Performance Meetings and Teams

Group Presentation Skills

Kids Day Training of Trainers

School-Community Partnership Building

Event Facilitation

Parent Summit

Kids Day

Student Leadership Summit

NTA IN THE EDUCATIONAL SETTING

YES (Youth Empowering Systems) is the name given to NTA's team approach within schools, and its foundation is the development and maintenance of the student assistance program. In the YES trainings, NTA helps educators design a program that promotes general wellness and encourages school personnel to become aware sooner of students experiencing personal distress. Building resiliency and enhancing protective factors are key ingredients in this empowerment process.

Program graduates report a sense of renewed dedication to the task of helping young people, a belief that change is possible, and a feeling of hope for the future. As a result of NTA's trainings in rural and urban areas throughout the United States, more than 2000 campuses are providing effective prevention and intervention programs for students.

NTA IN THE COMMUNITY SETTING

Whether economic, environmental, or social, the challenges facing communities call out for broad-based community collaboration and the integrated focusing of limited resources. Successful collaborations are the result of many variables, but three things are essential:

- A shared community perception of need

- The ability to collaborate

- People willing and able to become leaders

NTA offers a comprehensive consultation and training program for individuals, agencies, and businesses interested in forming community-based collaboratives. Entitled Building Community Partnerships, the program is designed to assist community-based teams develop and implement comprehensive plans that address such issues as violence prevention, mentoring, job training, economic development, community planning, and community-based programs for youth.

NTA IN THE BUSINESS SETTING

As part of its goal of promoting generational wellness for children, NTA is assisting businesses forge partnerships with schools and communities. These partnerships include both profit and nonprofit organizations, with particular focus on the establishment of collaboratives, work transitions, and mentor training. In addition, and specific to the business sector, NTA provides vision formation and strategic planning, leadership development, conflict management, meeting and retreat facilitation, organizational needs assessment, employee empowerment and productivity improvement, and communication skill building.

For more information regarding National Training Associates and their trainings and services, call or write:

National Training Associates
P.O. Box 1270
Sebastopol, CA 95473
(800) 624-1120 from outside California
(707) 829-1884 from inside California